# A Stranger in My Own House:

## The Story of

# W. E. B. Du Bois

# A Stranger in My Own House:

## The Story of

# W. E. B. Du Bois

Bonnie Hinman

**MORGAN REYNOLDS**
*Publishing, Inc.*

620 South Elm Street, Suite 223
Greensboro, North Carolina  27406
http://www.morganreynolds.com

# Portraits of
# Black Americans

Bayard Rustin
A. Philip Randolph
Roy Wilkins
W. E. B. Du Bois
Gwendolyn Brooks
Marcus Garvey
William Grant Still
Richard Wright
Thurgood Marshall
Langston Hughes
John Coltrane

A STRANGER IN MY OWN HOUSE: THE STORY OF W. E. B. DU BOIS

Copyright © 2005 by Bonnie Hinman

Library of Congress Cataloging-in-Publication Data

Hinman, Bonnie.
A stranger in my own house : the story of W.E.B. Du Bois / Bonnie
Hinman.—1st ed.
p. cm.
Includes bibliographical references and index.
ISBN 13: 978-1-931798-45-7
ISBN 1-931798-45-1 (alk. paper)
1. Du Bois, W. E. B. (William Edward Burghardt), 1868-1963—Juvenile
literature. 2. African Americans—Biography—Juvenile literature. 3. African
American intellectuals—Biography—Juvenile literature. 4. African American
civil rights workers—Biography—Juvenile literature. 5. National Association
for the Advancement of Colored People—Biography—Juvenile literature. 6.
African Americans—Civil rights—History—Juvenile literature. I. Title.
E185.97.D73H56 2005
305.896'073'0092—dc22

2004026460

Printed in the United States of America
First Edition

# Contents

# One

# A Challenging Start

When William Edward Burghardt Du Bois graduated from high school in Great Barrington, Massachusetts, in 1884, he was the only black student among the thirteen graduates. Each student gave a speech at the ceremony. William spoke about Wendell Phillips, a famous white abolitionist who had died the previous February. In 1836, Phillips had left his law practice to devote his life to fighting against slavery. He was an accomplished orator and traveled the country speaking passionately in favor of abolition. After President Abraham Lincoln issued the Emancipation Proclamation and the states ratified the Thirteenth Amendment, which prohibited slavery, Phillips continued to agitate for social reform, including women's voting rights.

*Opposite:* W. E. B. Du Bois *(Courtesy of National Portrait Gallery / Art Resource.)*

The Great Barrington High School class of 1884. Du Bois, the only African-American student, is at the far left. *(Special Collections and Archives, W.E.B. Du Bois Library, University of Massachusetts Amherst)*

Later, Du Bois could not remember if he had picked his own topic or had agreed to a teacher's suggestion, but he said: "I was fascinated by [Phillips's] life and his work and took a long step toward a wider conception of what I was going to do." William was just sixteen when he finished high school, but he had already begun the work that would occupy the rest of his long life.

Wendell Phillips's life represented the kind of accomplishments William admired. Phillips had graduated from Harvard and advocated for the rights of workers and for economic opportunity as well as for the end of slavery. Phillips spoke out tirelessly against oppression and in favor of freedom. But Phillips was white. Before

young William Du Bois could achieve the life he dreamed of, he would have to find a way around the problems of being born poor and black in the 1860s in America.

Born on Febrary 23, 1868, in an isolated, largely white community in western Massachusetts, William had a unique perspective on the problems of

The abolitionist Wendell Phillips.

race and Reconstruction that dominated America socially and politically. He was raised to believe that hard work was the key to economic success, which could buy not just material rewards but the refinement and intellectual life that were for him the hallmarks of admirable people.

His mother's family, the Burghardts, had lived in Massachusetts since the 1700s. Mary, William's mother, was one of ten children born into the farming family. Mary's husband, Alfred Du Bois (pronounced *Doo Boys*), was the descendant of a family that had emigrated from France to New York in the 1600s. Alfred's father, Alexander,

Mary Burghardt Du Bois with her young son William.
*(Special Collections and Archives, W.E.B. Du Bois Library, University of Massachusetts Amherst)*

was actually born in Haiti but grew up in the States and attended a private school in Connecticut. He went on to own a grocery store, work as a steward on a passenger boat, and farm. He had at least four wives and several children. One of those children, also born in Haiti, was Alfred Du Bois.

Alexander's children remembered him as a hard and unyielding man. Alfred reacted to his father's domineering style of child rearing by leaving home at a young age. Eventually, his travels brought him to Great Barrington, where he met and courted Mary Burghardt.

Much of what is known about W. E. B. Du Bois's early years and ancestry comes from his own stories. When his parents met, his mother already had a young son, Adelbert, but Du Bois offers almost no other information about this half brother. He remembered his father fondly: "He was small and beautiful of face and feature, just tinted with the sun, his wavy hair chiefly revealing his kinship to Africa. In nature, I think, he was a dreamer—romantic, indolent, kind, unreliable."

Alfred seems to have had some money when he arrived in Great Barrington because there is no evidence that he held a job while he and Mary lived together. But soon after William's birth, Alfred returned to his wandering ways. He may have left to find a job elsewhere with the intention of sending for his family, or he may have simply left. Whatever his reason, he was never to return.

William's father, Alfred Du Bois. *(Special Collections and Archives, W.E.B. Du Bois Library, University of Massachusetts Amherst.)*

Because of ill health, Mary had to rely on her family for help. Fortunately for William and his brother, the large Burghardt clan was close-knit and willing to pitch in. Though the family was poor, there was always enough to eat and clothes to wear and a few treats.

There were less than fifty African Americans in Great Barrington. Many of them had lived in the community their whole lives, as had their parents. Though they weren't necessarily accepted into white society as equals, blacks and whites attended school and church together, shopped in the same stores, and crossed paths often in day-to-day life. Western Massachusetts was a relatively safe place for a black child to grow up in the middle 1800s.

William attended the Great Barrington School, where he was the only African American in his class. He was an excellent student. William spent weekends and summers with white playmates as they roamed the surrounding hills, swimming in the summers, sledding in the winters, and occasionally getting into trouble. He played with the white boys, ate with them, and visited in their homes. It was an ordinary life for a boy of the time, but William was always aware that he was different.

The Burghardts were New Englanders in their customs and ways of looking at the world. Like many of their neighbors, they valued hard work, neatness, and orderliness. In a twist echoing the times, blacks and whites shared prejudices against the impoverished Irish and Germans who moved to town to work in the local woolen

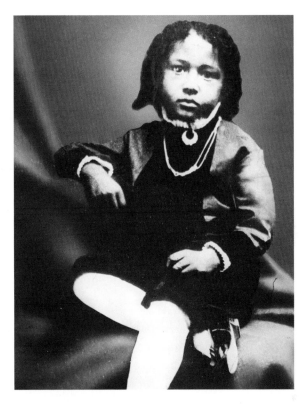

William Du Bois at age four. *(Special Collections and Archives, W.E.B. Du Bois Library, University of Massachusetts Amherst)*

mills. William wrote later that he looked down upon these people and their families.

William's mother instilled in him the idea that hard work was the key to success. She told him to learn all he could so he would be treated with respect. When William entered high school, his grades were so good that the principal suggested he take college preparatory classes. Despite his academic success, William's high school career was sometimes difficult. His mother suffered a stroke which partially crippled her. She worked when she could, and William took on odd jobs to help. The Burghardt aunts and uncles pitched in, and sometimes there was discreet help from white community members. William retreated a little into himself during this time, becoming more conscious of his family's poverty and his own inability to do anything about it. Having to take handouts made him unhappy, and he had few outlets for his feelings. Church and family events made up the social life that existed in Great Barrington.

One of the highlights of William's teenage years came when he was fifteen. He was invited to visit his grandfather, Alexander Du Bois, and Alexander's fourth wife. Mary was excited for her son to meet his grandfather, and perhaps hoped the elder Du Bois might help with William's education. Somehow she raised the money to send William on the train to New Bedford, Massachusetts.

Alexander Du Bois was retired and lived in relative comfort, but retained the prickly nature of his younger days. William found that his grandfather, though polite, talked little. He felt more welcomed by Alexander's wife, Annie, who introduced William to their circle of friends in New Bedford. The young man was overwhelmed at first. The people in Great Barrington were plainspoken. They were suspicious of grand behavior and ceremony. The people William met in New Bedford, by contrast, were much more formal.

More than seventy years later, William still had vivid memories of the day one of his grandfather's friends came to visit: "They sat down and talked seriously;

finally my grand-
father arose, filled
the wineglasses
and raised his glass
and touched the
glass of his friend,
murmuring a toast.
I had never before
seen such cer-
emony: I had read
about it in books,
but in Great
Barrington both
white and black
avoided ceremony.

William's paternal grandfather, Alexander Du Bois.

To them it smacked of pretense. . . . The black Burghardts
indulged in jokes and backslapping. I suddenly sensed
in my Grandfather's parlor what manners meant and how
people of breeding behaved and were able to express
what we in Great Barrington were loath to give act to,
or unable. I never forgot that toast."

The experience reinforced William's growing belief
that class differences were more significant than racial
ones. Having never before encountered up close the
manners and habits of people like his grandfather, William found himself attracted to their way of life. He
began to realize that the people he knew in Great
Barrington were not the only ones in the world—that
there were other ways and other places to live.

He had another eye-opening experience on his way home, when he spent the night in Providence, Rhode Island, with a friend of Annie Du Bois. This friend took William to the annual picnic at Rocky Point on Narragansett Bay. African Americans from three states gathered there each summer. William had seldom seen more than a few black people in one place. Here there were hundreds of men and women. William was both thrilled and amazed by the sight. He became even more keenly aware of how sheltered and isolated his own upbringing had been.

One of the ways William sought expression was through the written word. While still in high school he found a job selling the *New York Globe,* which later became the *New York Age.* The *Globe* was a pioneering newspaper that offered national news and some local news from dozens of correspondents. It served African Americans across the northeast United States. Soon William was writing a weekly report for the *Globe* about events in Great Barrington.

More than anything, William wanted to get out into the world and go to college. His family supported his dream, but college was expensive. Once again, the close-knit community of Great Barrington would have to rally together to find a way to support one of their own.

The obvious choice for college for William was Harvard University, which was in Cambridge, Massachusetts. Harvard, Wendell Phillips's alma mater, was the best school in the area—maybe even the country—and

William, like most other bright New Englanders, longed to go there. But Harvard was very expensive, and people worried William's high school education may not have adequately prepared him for its rigorous academics.

Friends advised William to work and study for a year and plan to enter college in the fall of 1885. He was only sixteen—he had plenty of time. William was impatient to get on with his life, but he realized patience might be prudent. He also had his mother to worry about. He felt obligated to help supplement her meager income. So he resigned himself to a year of work to prepare himself for his future.

In March of 1885, Mary Du Bois died suddenly of a stroke. William said later that his feelings were decidedly mixed about his mother's death. He mourned her passing but was glad that she was finally at peace. Uncomfortably, Mary's death was in some ways a boon because it released William from the responsibility he felt towards her: "Now I was free and unencumbered and at the same time more alone than I had ever dreamed of being. This very grief was a challenge. Now especially I must succeed as my mother so desperately wanted me to."

After Mary's death, William was taken in by an aunt and informally adopted by the entire African-American community of Great Barrington. Frank Hosmer, William's principal at the high school, sought to find a way to send his star pupil to college. He enlisted three other men in town, all white, and between them they convinced four

Congregationalist churches to each pledge one hundred dollars toward William Du Bois's college expenses.

Four hundred dollars was quite a bit of money at the time, but it was not enough for Harvard. The sting of William's disappointment was alleviated by the news that he would be able to attend college at Fisk University, an all-black school in Nashville, Tennessee. Fisk had a good reputation and Du Bois was intrigued by its location: "I was going into the South; the South of slavery, rebellion, and black folk; above all, I was going to meet colored people of my own age and education, of my own ambitions."

# Two

# New Horizons

William's family and friends worried that going south to attend college was a step backward. Conditions for African Americans in the South were deplorable, and Nashville was no exception.

In the years following the Civil War, the nation as a whole faced difficult problems: how to integrate free African Americans, including former slaves, into the general population; and how to begin to rebuild the devastated South and bring the Union together once more. Initially, the federal government imposed sanctions on Southern states that forced the white power structure to cede its influence to African Americans and radical Republicans—a period known as Reconstruction, which was overseen and enforced by federal soldiers.

Though Reconstruction had good intentions and made some impressive achievements—including the election of hundreds of black men to state and national office, and the creation of free and integrated public schools— it met with stiff and determined resistance. Corruption, a general weakening of support for radical leaders throughout the country, and the activities of terrorist groups such as the Ku Klux Klan led to the overthrow of most of the progressive governments. The disputed presidential election of 1876 was resolved when the victor, Rutherford B. Hayes, promised to complete the withdrawal of federal troops from the South.

This print from 1872 shows the first African Americans elected to the U.S. Congress: Robert C. De Large, Jefferson H. Long, H. R. Revels, Benjamin S. Turner, Josiah T. Walls, Joseph H. Rainy, and R. Brown Elliot.

THE FIRST COLORED SENATOR AND REPRESENTATIVES.

In the 41ˢᵗ and 42ⁿᵈ Congress of the United States.

The last two decades of the nineteenth century saw a decline of the political and social achievements made by Reconstruction. The post-Reconstruction South was a region ruled by bitterness and fear. Though two Constitutional amendments had

President Rutherford B. Hayes. *(National Portrait Gallery, Washington, D.C.)*

been ratified that guaranteed citizenship, due process, equal protection under the law (the Fourteenth, in 1868), and the right to vote to all men regardless of color (the Fifteenth, in 1870), states across the South began enacting a series of laws that were designed to thwart blacks from exercising their new rights. These laws eventually became known as Jim Crow laws, named for a minstrel show character that performed a degrading routine.

Fisk Free Colored School opened in 1865, the year the Civil War ended, and became Fisk University two years later. It was devoted to educating newly freed slaves. During Reconstruction, Fisk sent hundreds of graduates into teaching positions and helped hundreds of other students to get access to education. When Reconstruction ended and the Jim Crow era began, Fisk continued its mission to educate African-American students.

By 1885, the South that Du Bois headed into was a dangerous place for a young black man. Jim Crow laws covered all aspects of life. There were laws preventing black school children from using books white children might touch. There were laws forcing separate entrances for whites and blacks to hospitals; separate waiting rooms in those hospitals; separate seats on buses or trains; separate water fountains, libraries, barbers, prisons, mental institutions, toilets; and even separate public parks. The result was that black people in the South lived in a highly restricted, highly combustible world. If they were tired, they had to think twice before sitting on a park bench. If they were hungry, they had to find a restaurant that would serve them. If they wanted to travel, they had to find a place that would house them. If they violated any Jim Crow law, they could be beaten or killed. If they made it to the relative safety of jail, black inmates were represented by white lawyers, judged by white juries, and sentenced by white judges.

Many Southern states gradually enacted a series of laws that effectively kept blacks from voting by imposing poll taxes and literacy requirements—caveats enforced only for black votes, not poor or illiterate whites. These deterrents, combined with the threat of physical violence, worked to keep most African Americans away from the voting booth, and meant no black representatives were elected.

Further, despite the Fourteenth Amendment's promise of equal protection under the law, African Americans were routinely victimized by the legal system. Blacks were barred from serving on juries, and their legal representation was often biased or ineffective. Because of systemic prejudice, African Americans were often arrested and tried for crimes they did not commit, or that were not actually crimes. This led to a system called peonage. African Americans were arrested and convicted of some minor crime—regardless of the truth. They were then leased out to white farmers or business owners to work off their sentences.

African-American farmers were subjected to cheating by high interest rates, crop-lien laws, and fraudulent accounting by the landlord and the company store. Every single local law and custom worked to keep the farmers from providing for their families no matter how hard they labored.

The summer before William left for college he was hired as a timekeeper at a building site in Great Barrington. A wealthy widow had begun the building of a great blue granite mansion. Du Bois was paid the substantial sum of a dollar a day to keep track of the workers' time.

His earnings allowed him to purchase some new clothes and otherwise prepare for his upcoming adventure. In September of 1885, having packed his few possessions and said his good-byes, William Du Bois climbed on the train for Tennessee. On the way he met another young man traveling to Fisk who proposed that the two be roommates. Du Bois agreed. He and his new friend, Otho Porter, spent the rest of the trip talking and laughing, sharing their excitement, and trying to hide their apprehension about the future.

Du Bois had not experienced the kind of day-in and day-out racism that was the norm to those familiar with the area, so it was upsetting to him to learn how black people were treated. He was particularly shocked by the open contempt white people showed toward blacks.

In contrast, Du Bois found Fisk and its campus almost intoxicating. The school was a bastion of learning and, at least while on campus, Du Bois was treated with the respect and engagement he longed for. He was several years younger than most of the other students, and he was from New England, which was unusual. His grades from high school were so high that he was admitted to Fisk as a sophomore. Though academically prepared to succeed, Du Bois required time to adjust to life in this new world.

The Fisk University campus in the mid-1880s. *(Library of Congress)*

Du Bois's New England reticence and dedication to hard work made him seem bookish and shy to those around him. Having grown up in the sheltered and reserved world of tiny Great Barrington, Du Bois was stunned by the vibrant social scene at Fisk. Du Bois later wrote, "Never before had I seen young men so self-assured and who gave themselves such airs, and colored men at that; and above all for the first time I saw beautiful girls." He recalled that he lost his appetite for supper the first night in the dining hall when he saw all the pretty young women around him. Du Bois had never dated a girl, and once this fact became known his dorm mates were eager to fix him up. He was terrified by the prospect. His shyness was often misinterpreted as a kind of aloofness, so he sometimes had trouble making friends. Being young and far from home and a stranger to the South, Du Bois felt more comfortable keeping close to himself and his books. When pushed, he chose to pretend a confidence that was largely superficial. But those who did get to know the quiet young man would discover his wit, his intelligence, and most of all his desire to make a difference in the world.

Fisk was a community in itself largely separated from the city of Nashville. Most Fisk students stayed close to campus. Though the campus was a comfortable and happy place, the world outside was not always as friendly.

One day, when Du Bois was in Nashville, he accidentally jostled a white woman he passed on the street. He instinctively and immediately raised his hat and begged her pardon. Despite his apology, the woman's reaction struck him to the core: "The woman was furious; why I never knew; somehow, I cannot say how, I had transgressed the interracial mores of the South. Was it because I showed no submissiveness? Did I fail to debase myself utterly and eat spiritual dirt? Did I act as equals among equals? I do not know. I only sensed scorn and hate; the kind of despising, which a dog might incur."

The woman's reaction was not only confusing to Du Bois but it was also insulting and upsetting. From that moment on he resolved to avoid situations that might cause those feelings. His pride was deeply wounded by this woman's rage at his touch, so he became careful to interact with white people as little as possible. He tried not to make eye contact with, stand near, or speak to a white person if he could avoid it.

Du Bois's knowledge of slavery meant he was already predisposed to hate injustice and any system that oppressed its people, but incidents like this one and the countless others he witnessed or heard about from friends touched him deeply. He directed his fury into his work, studying even harder. He was determined to learn all he could about the world and use that knowledge to help fight segregation and discrimination. He wasn't sure yet just how he would help people, but he was certain that education was the key.

During two summer vacations from Fisk, Du Bois chose to go to east Tennessee to teach at a school for poor African-American children. As he later explained, "I had heard about the country in the South as the real seat of slavery. I wanted to know it."

After a short stint at a teacher-training facility where prospective summer teachers brushed up on fractions and spelling and other basics, the teachers were sent out to look for jobs. Du Bois walked from community to community asking if the residents needed a teacher. In some places it had been years since school had been held.

Du Bois settled in with an African-American community that welcomed the young teacher eagerly. The schoolhouse was a log hut that a farmer had used to store corn. There were rough plank benches and a rickety desk for the teacher. There was no blackboard and few books. Du

Du Bois's contract to teach school to the children and grandchildren of ex-slaves in rural Tennessee. *(Special Collections and Archives, W.E.B. Du Bois Library, University of Massachusetts Amherst)*

Bois saw in the poor little school the South that he had searched for.

Du Bois taught in the school for two summers. He taught the children spelling and reading, and they taught him to sing the old African-American spirituals called the sorrow songs. He visited them in their homes, shared their meals, and visited their churches. His education at Fisk was made complete by his summers in east Tennessee.

Graduation approached in spring of 1888, and Du Bois, emboldened by his success, began to think about continuing his education—at Harvard. He applied and was accepted if he would enter as a junior rather than a graduate student. Du Bois didn't care what his status was as long as he was going to be studying at the school

Du Bois, seated left, with the Fisk graduating class of 1888. *(Special Collections and Archives, W.E.B. Du Bois Library, University of Massachusetts Amherst)*

of his dreams. His excellent grades at Fisk earned him a scholarship, which made it possible for his dreams to finally come true.

After graduation from Fisk, Du Bois and some classmates worked at a summer hotel at Lake Minnetonka near Minneapolis. Though Du Bois had never worked as a waiter before, he managed to earn a little money. The group earned more at the end of the summer when they performed a series of concerts as a glee club. Du Bois, ever dedicated and organized, acted as their business manager and arranged the concerts.

In September, Du Bois left for Harvard. He found a comfortable room to rent in a home in a quiet African-American neighborhood. To his surprise, he discovered that the racial tension he experienced in the South also existed in the North. In Cambridge, Massachusetts, it was a quiet, less emotional rejection—though a rejection all the same. Du Bois again took refuge in an internal life of study. He paid little attention to the social life of the university, knowing he would not be welcome in the white world of clubs and associations. He did try out for the Glee Club, because he had a good singing voice, but he was not invited to join: "I ought to have known that Harvard could not afford to have a black on its Glee Club traveling about the country. Quite naturally I was rejected."

Du Bois's experience in Tennessee had convinced him that racism was the norm and that he would be better off if he accepted that rather than becoming angry or

This hand-colored photomechanical print from the 1890s shows the main gate that leads into Harvard Yard on the prestigious campus. *(Library of Congress)*

discouraged each time he encountered it. All Du Bois wanted from the school was to learn from its professors and to have access to the library as he prepared himself for a career in philosophy. He discovered that, in his opinion, the teachers at Harvard were not necessarily better than the ones he had at Fisk, but they were better known and had better facilities to help in the pursuit of knowledge.

Du Bois did have friends—mostly other African-American students or residents of Boston or other nearby towns: "With them I led a happy and inspiring life. There were among them many educated and well-to-do folk; many young people studying or planning to study; many charming young women. We met and ate, danced and argued and planned a new world." He would later re-

W. E. B. Du Bois during his time at Harvard. *(Special Collections and Archives, W.E.B. Du Bois Library, University of Massachusetts Amherst)*

member having been happy at Harvard—not in spite of his isolation, but because of it. Du Bois knew that his approach was no final solution to racial problems, but it enabled him to navigate the world of Harvard success-fully.

One of the ideas Du Bois explored at Harvard was that discrimination was based on ignorance. He became convinced that if each race could learn and understand the truth about the other, they would have no reason to hate or fear. Du Bois knew himself to be no different than the white students who looked right through him on campus. He had to believe that if they could only realize that, they would stop pretending he did not exist.

One way the system of slavery had been explained and condoned for many years was by claiming that African Americans were genetically inferior and actually benefited from slavery because they would not be able to care for themselves or their families if left to their own devices. Even after slavery ended, African Americans continued to be viewed as less civilized, less intelligent, less cultivated, and more prone to violence and crime than white citizens.

Du Bois was certain that these harmful stereotypes could be eradicated through education. In the meantime, he remained apart from his white peers. Though he would later admit that he was rather self-centered during his student days and had a sharp tongue, he also said that part of his aloofness was caused by a fear that these students would reject or humiliate him. It was better not to take the risk. He convinced himself that he was happy in his own world of library, classroom, and black friends.

At Harvard, Du Bois's belief in voluntary racial segregation was solidified. Because he felt more comfortable and more valued when he was not trying to fit into what he felt was a white man's world, he came to the conclusion that African Americans would be better off in their own communities, where they could offer each

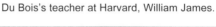

other the support and encouragement the outside world would not. Du Bois's conviction that segregation could be good for African Americans was not a mainstream idea for a black intellectual. Du Bois later admitted, "I was, however, exceptional among Negroes in my ideas on voluntary race segregation; they for the most part saw salvation only in integration at the earliest moment and on almost any terms in white culture; I was firm in my criticism of white folk and in my dream of a Negro self-sufficient culture even in America."

While at Harvard, Du Bois studied with the famous philosopher William James. Though he was one of James's most prized students, he clashed with his teacher over the theory of pragmatism. James argued that incremental changes were the only ones possible in the real world. Du Bois took the position that radical changes had to be possible. James said that people could only make changes to their world based on their very limited knowledge of it, but Du Bois believed that people

Du Bois's teacher at Harvard, William James.

could make changes based on what they wanted their world to become. Though Du Bois's philosophy would continue to develop, his basic optimism and conviction that a better world was possible would not desert him.

In June of 1890, Du Bois graduated with honors from Harvard with a bachelor's degree in philosophy. He was one of five graduates selected to speak at the commencement exercises. Du Bois later wrote of that occasion, "My subject was Jefferson Davis. I chose it with deliberate intent of facing Harvard and the nation with a discussion of slavery as illustrated in the person of the president of the Confederate States of America. Naturally my effort made a sensation."

Du Bois's speech was shocking because in it he praised Davis, speaking of him as "a naturally brave and generous man." Du Bois wanted to make the point that Davis himself was not a bad man, even though he fought a war in order to win the right to continue the oppression of an entire race. Du Bois was trying to show the reason Davis did so was a result of the civilization he lived in and its influences—not necessarily of his natural inclinations.

Several periodicals of the time printed positive remarks or reviews of the speech. *The New York Nation* said, "Du Bois handled his difficult and hazardous subject with absolute good taste, great moderation, and almost contemptuous fairness." Other people reacted more tentatively, wondering what to make of Du Bois's assertions. It would not be the first time his remarks were met with some confusion.

Upon graduation from Harvard, Du Bois hoped to become a professor of philosophy. But William James reminded him such jobs would be difficult to come by. Du Bois had studied a good deal of history, especially the history of blacks in America, and decided to try to combine those two fields together. He would use the precepts of philosophy to try to understand the history of African Americans. He applied and was accepted to Harvard's graduate school, where he received a full scholarship.

Du Bois's graduate thesis, or paper, which Harvard would publish as the first of a new history series in 1896, was titled *The Suppression of the African Slave-Trade to the United States of America, 1638-1870*. The book is still used today to research that era of African-American history. In this chronological history of slave trading in the United States, Du Bois details attitudes and actions in the United States and internationally that contributed to the suppression of, or failure to suppress, the slave trade. Much of Du Bois's later research and writing can be traced back to this first book. His interest in international causes and events and his desire to educate in a dispassionate manner, using statistics and other incontrovertible data, have their roots in *The Suppression of the African Slave-Trade*. In this book, Du Bois took his first steps into the developing field of sociology.

Sociology was a relatively new field, one that proposed to study human groups and their interactions. It

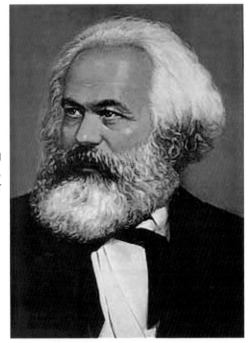

The father of communism and a huge influence on Du Bois, economist and philosopher Karl Marx.

appealed to Du Bois because it combined his love of scientific research and his fondness for statistics with his interest in understanding the divide between the races. One of the most influential people on this developing field was the thinker Karl Marx, who argued that class divisions—which, for him, were inextricably linked to economic divisions—had the biggest impact on social change. Marx also suggested that it was possible to study history scientifically, an idea that Du Bois's logical mind found compelling.

Marx's theories appealed to Du Bois because he remembered the differences he had noticed between the reserved New Englanders of Great Barrington and the people of his grandfather's circle. He could clearly see the distinctions class and economics made between people. But Du Bois took Marx's theories a step further. Looking at his own experiences through that lens, he realized the divide between blacks and whites was as tied to economics as it was to race. Though sociology was still a developing field, Du Bois saw in it the promise of understanding human interaction that he had been looking for since his years at Fisk. It also confirmed his thoughts about the importance of voluntary segregation. By deliberately supporting black businesses, African Americans could help each other begin to bridge the class and racial divide.

After two years of graduate school at Harvard, Du Bois saw the next logical step in his education as studying in Germany. There he could have better access to the work of philosophers, including Marx and other economic and sociological thinkers. Harvard had no more scholarships or fellowships for him so Du Bois approached the Slater Fund, which had been established to help African-American scholars gain access to advanced education. The fund was administered by ex-president Rutherford B. Hayes. At first, Hayes said that the Slater Fund was no longer providing scholarships. Du Bois persisted and eventually convinced Hayes and the Slater Fund board to give him a $750 fellowship so he might study in Europe.

From the moment he stepped on the boat that would take him across the Atlantic, Du Bois felt as though he had entered another world. Racial discrimination was

The University of Berlin, where Du Bois studied from 1892-1894. *(Library of Congress)*

less prevalent in Germany and other European countries. Du Bois was amazed by the way people reacted— or rather, did not react—to him: "They did not always pause to regard me as a curiosity, or something sub-human; I was just a man of the somewhat privileged student rank, with whom they were glad to meet and talk over the world; particularly, the part of the world whence I came."

His time in Germany was a life-changing experience for Du Bois. He traveled freely, made white friends, and no longer had to protect himself from insults. He studied at the University of Berlin and traveled throughout Europe. His two years in Europe "modified profoundly" his outlook on life. He found a use for good manners and allowed himself to slow down enough to enjoy art and music. He was pleased to find that many Europeans shared his concerns about racial inequality in America and the unhealthy American obsession with making money.

Du Bois's intellectual development was strongly influenced by his studies in Berlin. He read more of Marx's theory and, while he claimed he did not fully understand it, he agreed with Marx that justice for everyone could not occur as long as there were vast disparities of wealth. Marxism was especially appealing to Du Bois because it confirmed his belief that economic inequality was at the root of racism. He began to think that change in American race relations might be possible through addressing economic injustice.

On his twenty-fifth birthday, Du Bois made a diary entry that shows his new-found optimism: "These are my plans: to make a name in science, to make a name in literature and thus to raise my race. Or perhaps to raise a visible empire in Africa through England, France or Germany. I wonder what will be the outcome? Who knows?"

These are the words of a young man ready to make his way in the world. It must have been tempting to think of staying in Europe, where life would be so much easier. But in 1894, at the end of his two years of study, Du Bois boarded a ship and started for home. Armed with his new ideas, he believed he could make an impact on the problems of race in America.

# Three

# Finding His Place

Du Bois returned to a country that had severe economic problems. By the end of 1893, nearly 15,000 companies failed and five hundred banks went into receivership. The panic of 1893 had plunged the country into a three-year depression. Times were tough and money was tight. It was not a good environment in which to be looking for a job.

Du Bois later explained his approach to job seeking: "I was not exacting or hard to please. I just got down on my knees and begged for work." He wrote application letters for months, starting with what he considered the most desirable schools for African-American students. Howard University, Hampton Institute, Tuskegee Institute, and Fisk had no openings. At last, a few offers dribbled in. Du Bois accepted the first, which was made

Wilberforce University, the institution where Du Bois began his teaching career, in the late nineteenth century. *(Library of Congress)*

by Wilberforce University in Ohio. He traveled there in August 1894.

Wilberforce was a small school administered by the African Methodist Episcopal Church with the help of some funding from the state. Du Bois was initially hired to teach Latin and Greek, but eventually taught English and German, too. Times were such that every teacher had to pitch in wherever he could.

The conservative religious philosophy of Wilberforce was at the heart of every aspect of the college; Du Bois managed to run afoul of that philosophy more than once. Soon after his arrival on campus, he wandered into a student prayer meeting. Upon seeing him, the student leader immediately announced that Professor Du Bois would lead the group in prayer. The professor just as quickly replied, "No he won't." An uproar followed and Du Bois almost lost his new job. Fortunately for him, he was able to explain that he just was not prepared to be asked to lead a prayer session and he was eventually forgiven.

In truth, Du Bois took issue with the religious culture at Wilberforce. He thought that the regular revivals and many mandatory church services took time and energy away from the educational mission of the school. He was also unable to persuade the administration at Wilberforce to allow him to teach a class in sociology. Compared to the atmosphere of intellectual curiosity that had been encouraged at Harvard and in Germany, Wilberforce felt sluggish. He later explained, "I went to Wilberforce with high ideals. I wanted to help build a great university. I was willing to work night as well as day, and taught full time. I helped in student discipline, took part in the social life, and began to write books. But I found myself against a stone wall. Nothing stirred before my impatient pounding! Or if it stirred, it soon slept again."

In spite of his frustrations, Du Bois was building a solid career at Wilberforce. Harvard awarded him a PhD in philosophy in 1896, based on the work he had done there and on his doctoral thesis, which was published that same year.

During his second year at Wilberforce, Du Bois fell in love with a beautiful woman who had come from

Cedar Rapids, Iowa, to study at the university. Nina Gomer was Du Bois's student, and she was remembered by her peers as a bright, fun, and happy young woman. Du Bois had begun to think about marriage, and when he met Nina, he was taken by her kindness and enjoyment of life.

Du Bois's wife, Nina Gomer Du Bois.

After a brief courtship, the couple was married at Nina's home in Iowa in May of 1896. They then returned to a two-room apartment in the men's dormitory at Wilberforce. But Du Bois was not happy about the prospect of another year at that school and was delighted to receive a job offer from the University of Pennsylvania.

The offer was for a temporary appointment as an assistant instructor of sociology at what Du Bois considered to be a paltry salary of nine hundred dollars a year. Though he was insulted by the money, he was so glad to be free of Wilberforce he accepted the position immediately.

The job in Pennsylvania was intriguing. Du Bois would not be teaching classes. Instead, he was granted a special fellowship to conduct a study of the black community in Philadelphia's Seventh Ward slums. A university official, Charles Harrison, outlined the project this way: "We want to know precisely how this class of people live; what occupations they follow; from what occupations they are excluded; how many of their children go to school; and to ascertain every fact which will throw light on this social problem."

Du Bois and Nina moved to a single room apartment over a cafeteria in the worst slum of Philadelphia. The newlyweds made the best of their circumstances, which were extremely different from the quiet life they knew in Ohio. Du Bois said that their neighborhood was "in the slums where kids played intriguing games like 'cops and lady bums'; and where in the night when pistols popped, you didn't get up lest you find you couldn't."

The Seventh Ward was considered to be a hotbed of criminal activity. This might have gone unremarked if the Seventh Ward had not also been home to a number of wealthy white families who pressured the government to do something about the crime problem. As Du Bois put it more cynically, Philadelphia was having one of its "periodic spasms of reform." Caught up in the spirit of reform beginning to take hold of the country, the University of Pennsylvania agreed to sponsor a study of the black population of the Seventh Ward in an effort to learn about its problems and to determine what, if anything, could be done to improve the situation.

The late nineteenth century saw the beginning of what became known as the Progressive movement. Generally centered in urban areas, progressivism voiced concerns about human rights and looked for ways to help people out of the challenges brought about by poverty. People like Jane Addams of Hull House went into poor neighborhoods to live and work and try to find ways to better the lives of the people there.

The Philadelphia appointment gave Du Bois the opportunity to begin testing his belief that blacks suffered discrimination at the hands of whites because there was little understanding between the races. He proposed that discrimination would cease once whites learned that most of what they believed about blacks was false. He hoped the Philadelphia study would be a good place to gather facts to support his hypothesis. He was not blind to the fact that his race was one of the reasons he was selected for the job. The study's backers believed that any criticism would best come from a black man. Du Bois chose to look past this motive in order to do the work he believed in.

In keeping with his belief in the importance of hard data, Du Bois began a careful block-by-block survey. He used local libraries for research as he mapped the district. He classified the district by conditions and compiled a history of the black community in Philadelphia stretching back nearly two hundred years. He spoke with over 5,000 people.

By the late nineteenth century, Philadelphia was a sprawling city facing many modern urban issues such as high crime rates, overcrowding, and pollution. *(Library of Congress)*

At first, the residents of the Seventh Ward did not like being studied. But Du Bois persisted, and what he found surprised him. His first discovery was that he knew much less about his race than he had previously thought: "First of all I became painfully aware that merely being born in a group, does not necessarily make one possessed of complete knowledge concerning it. I had learned far more from Philadelphia Negroes than I had taught them concerning the Negro Problem." Though it meant questioning his own beliefs and assumptions, Du Bois pressed on in his quest. He was determined to find out as much he could in order to produce the most complete and comprehensive study of African Americans ever undertaken.

The study was published by the University of Pennsylvania in 1899 as *The Philadelphia Negro*. At nearly one thousand pages, Du Bois's work was full of revelations about the black community that went distinctly against commonly held beliefs. The revelation that there were different social classes within the African-American community was a new idea—most people tended to think of blacks as one big group. Du Bois showed that, just as in any other society, there were clear divisions between middle-class, working-class, and poor African Americans. The study was also unique in that it considered the thoughts, feelings, beliefs, and desires of its subjects. Previously, most studies of African Americans had set out to confirm the author's hypothesis, not to test and revise it. Du Bois drew his conclusions from the evidence he gathered, not the other way around. Other studies done on the black population had used such bizarre science as the now outdated concept of physiognomy, which purported to be able to determine personality from facial characteristics, to "prove" that black people were genetically inferior and more prone to be criminals.

Du Bois's study revealed that the history of discrimination based on race had been a detriment to the development and success of African Americans. It also established clearly that the way whites and blacks interacted was detrimental to both groups. Du Bois's study was a careful, scholarly work, but it did not lead to any specific reforms in Philadelphia or anywhere else. Du Bois was frustrated, but he felt what he was doing was groundwork that had to be completed before substantial change could begin. Most importantly, he was proving beyond a doubt that economic disparity was at the root of the so-called Negro problem.

During the course of his research, Du Bois gave several speeches to organizations interested in learning more about his work. He published excerpts in several prominent magazines and journals. His work sparked a series of similar studies.

Du Bois wished he could be everywhere at once. In the meantime, he was being talked about across the country as an up-and-coming scholar. His talents did not escape the attention of the president of Atlanta University, Horace Bumstead. His university had begun a series of conferences on problems of urban blacks, and Bumstead thought Du Bois was the ideal person to direct the project.

President Bumstead had to convince the university trustees that a position should be offered to Du Bois. His scholarship wasn't called into question, but his religion, or lack thereof, was. It had become well known that Du Bois was independent minded when it came to his religious beliefs. Du Bois himself admitted that while he had been raised to believe in organized religion, by the time he went through Harvard and his training in Germany he had become more skeptical. Still, Bumstead managed to convince the trustees that Du Bois was the man for the job.

As Du Bois was hurrying to finish his work in Philadelphia, he and Nina had more good news. On October 2, 1897, Nina, who had been sent to Du Bois's family in Great Barrington, away from the dirty streets of the Seventh Ward, gave birth to a healthy baby boy. The proud parents named him Burghardt Gomer. This baby would first bring them joy, then be their undoing.

# Four

## Atlanta

Du Bois, Nina, and their baby arrived in Atlanta in the fall of 1897. They took rooms in the men's dormitory because the African-American neighborhood other professors lived in was far away. Here at last Du Bois would be teaching his beloved sociology, along with history, economics, political science, and statistics. He wrote later of this time, "My real life work was begun at Atlanta for 13 years, from my 29th to my 42nd birthday. They were years of great spiritual upturning, of the making and unmaking of ideals, of hard work and hard play. Here I found myself."

Du Bois enthusiastically took charge of the conferences, which had started just one year previously. The first conference had focused on the health problems of African Americans. Du Bois soon made an ambitious plan for the future. He wanted the emphasis of the conferences to be on collecting a basic body of information about the social condition of blacks in cities. The Atlanta studies had been somewhat tailored after similar conferences held at other universities that had concentrated on the agricultural and industrial problems of rural blacks.

The Atlanta conferences were planned in ten-year cycles. Each year's study would focus on one aspect of African-American life. Du Bois planned to study African-American-run businesses, churches, crime, and the social and physical conditions of people living in the cities. Each year's study would be published and made available to the public. Du Bois hoped to repeat the ten-

Atlanta University.

year cycle, gradually adding to the data and collecting a broad base of information about African Americans in cities.

The conferences were plagued by financial problems, but Du Bois found ways to keep the program afloat for sixteen years—from 1898 to 1913. Du Bois knew that the conferences and resulting publications would have limitations, but he was convinced that something greater than mere scholarship was being accomplished: "It must be remembered that the significance of these studies lay not so much in what they were actually able to accomplish, as in the fact that at the time of their publication Atlanta University was the only institution in the world carrying on a systematic study of the Negro and his development, and putting the result in a form available for the scholars of the world."

Du Bois's statement highlights one of the major criticisms of the work that he did in Atlanta: that it offered little immediate help to the victims of discrimination. But Du Bois was a scholar by training, and he firmly believed that information was power and would help lead to change.

One year before the Du Bois family had arrived in Atlanta, the United States Supreme Court had handed down its famous ruling in the case of *Plessy v. Ferguson.* In 1892, a Louisiana shoemaker named Homer Plessy was convinced by the Citizen's Committee to Test the Constitutionality of the Separate Car Law to challenge the railroad's policy of reserving a car for white people only. Plessy was one-eighth African American and he and his family lived as white citizens. But one month after boarding a whites-only railroad car, he was arrested for violating the Separate Car Act. The Citizen's Committee took up his defense, taking the case all the way to the Supreme Court, where they argued that Plessy's rights under the Thirteenth and Fourteenth Amendments had been violated. The judges disagreed in an eight-to-one ruling. They decided that states had the right to enforce separate-but-equal segregation within their own boundaries. This decision essentially opened the door to fifty years of legal segregation.

Now that Jim Crow laws had a legal precedent, they became more far-reaching than ever. Black people living in the Southern states were generally subject to an institutionalized racism that is difficult to comprehend from this historical distance.

It was in this environment that Du Bois worked. State law segregated the streetcars in Atlanta in 1891, and eventually even public parks were forbidden to blacks. Du Bois and his family stayed close to the university's campus. As at Fisk, Du Bois preferred that he and Nina avoid contact with local whites whenever possible. Nina stayed in their rooms while Du Bois remained in his office with his books and papers. Anyone who wanted to speak to him had to come to him. Du Bois later described the way he tackled living under a doctrine of "separate but equal": "I tried to isolate myself in the ivory tower of race. I wanted to explain the difficulties

William and Nina with their son Burghardt, not long before Burghardt's death.
*(Special Collections and Archives, W.E.B. Du Bois Library, University of Massachusetts Amherst)*

of race and the ways in which these difficulties caused political and economic troubles."

But Du Bois could not insulate himself from all the pain and suffering in the world, nor could he use his scientific mind to deal with every challenge. In the early spring of 1899, his son, Burghardt, became ill, probably with diphtheria, an often deadly bacterial infection. Because the infection can initially resemble the common cold, William and Nina did not decide to seek medical attention right away. When they did, they could not find a single hospital that would admit their child, because of the color of his skin. Burghardt was just two and a half when he died in May 1899.

"His death tore our lives in two," wrote Du Bois later. "I threw myself more completely into my work, while most reason for living left the soul of my wife. Another child, a girl, came later, but my wife never forgave God for the unhealable wound." Burghardt's death also added stress to an already fragile marriage. Nina and William were beginning to discover they had different goals and desires, and Burghardt's death drove them further apart.

The only solace Du Bois could find

W. E. B. Du Bois with his cane. *(Special Collections and Archives, W.E.B. Du Bois Library, University of Massachusetts Amherst)*

was in his work. He channeled his grief into his teaching and his studies. He was not initially a popular teacher, partly because he was not particularly outgoing and partly because he still affected the gloves and cane he had become accustomed to using in Germany. Many of his students associated the cane with beatings they had endured and were further put off by Du Bois's airs. But his classes were always full and he gradually gained a reputation as a smart and engaging teacher.

In addition to his class load, Du Bois was also occupied by supervising the conferences. He traveled a good deal to lecture about his research across the United States.

In 1900, Du Bois was invited to take an exhibit to the famous Paris Exposition. Designed to showcase the technological, social, and economic advances of the times, the Paris Exposition would ceremonially close the door on the previous century while ushering in the next. Thousands of delegates from all over the globe planned to attend, bringing with them the latest innovations and news from their countries. One of the United States' offerings to the fair was a section on African Americans. Thomas J. Calloway, a Fisk classmate of Du Bois who now worked for the War Department, was in charge of the entire American Negro Exhibit. He asked Du Bois to assemble exhibits from Georgia and several other Southern states.

Du Bois and several of his students put together a collection of photographs, charts, models, and other displays. In mid-June 1900, Du Bois and his many boxes of materials boarded a ship from New York. He was paid a small stipend for his efforts but said that it hardly covered his expenses.

The Paris Exposition Universelle was held on nearly three hundred acres stretching on both sides of the Seine River from the Eiffel Tower to the Place de la Concorde. Palatial buildings housed exhibits devoted to Arts and Letters, Agriculture, Hygiene, Education, and many others. Germany, Great Britain, and Russia had huge national pavilions. France had the Grand Palais and its sister, the Petit Palais.

The building that housed the American Negro Exhibit was plain white and bore the inscription "The Science of Society." Du Bois planned for his exhibit to display a sampling of the research being done for the Atlanta conferences. Part of his goal was to show his international audience that African Americans were not easily lumped into one large group. To that end, he assembled four volumes containing a total of 363 photographs of African Americans. The photos made it clear that race did not need to be the defining characteristic of the African American—the people in the pictures exhibited a wide range of shapes, sizes, colors, and markers of social class.

The exhibit won a grand prize, and Du Bois, as the compiler and author, won a gold medal. After this success, Du Bois traveled to London for a Pan-African Conference at the end of July. The term Pan-Africanism had been coined only a year before by the conference's organizer, Henry Sylvester Williams. Pan-Africanism was a worldwide movement to join all people of African descent together for mutual aid and protection. Thirty-one-year-old Williams was a lawyer who had been born in Trinidad, educated in Canada, and recently established in London.

Six American delegates attended the inaugural conference, including Du Bois and Thomas Calloway. Because so many distinguished people were there, the conference received a good deal of press coverage. Most of the speeches and papers presented in the

These photographs are just a few of the 363 images that Du Bois compiled into albums entitled "Types of American Negroes, Georgia, U.S.A." and "Negro Life in Georgia, U.S.A." and displayed at the 1900 Paris Exposition for the "American Negro" exhibit. *(Library of Congress)*

Westminster Town Hall made a generally moderate appeal for restraint among whites toward blacks rather than a call for rebellion.

Du Bois delivered his speech at the closing session of the conference. Titled "To the Nations of the World," it offered a succinct explanation of what Du Bois's research and experiences had led him to conclude: "The problem of the twentieth century is the problem of the color line." Beyond that, Du Bois went on to say that these color differences should not be "hereafter, the basis of denying over half the world the right of sharing to their utmost ability the opportunities and privileges of modern civilization." It was, Du Bois felt, that simple. The only problem was how to bridge gap. Du Bois, as always, believed education would help.

Du Bois returned home just in time to greet his new daughter, a healthy baby he and Nina named Yolande. She was born on October 21, 1900, and her birth went a little way toward healing the pain left behind by Burghardt's death.

Du Bois hoped that his successful Paris Exposition and his role in the Pan-African Conference would lead to more recognition and financial support for the Atlanta Conferences. When the expected financial help didn't materialize, Du Bois had to struggle to complete the research on an ever-shrinking budget. Despite the dwindling support for his work, he still held fast to the basic belief that the world would want to know the truth about African Americans and needed only the accuracy of his studies to sway their opinions. He would later say, "This was, of course, but a young man's idealism, not by any means false, but also never universally true."

Eventually, Du Bois began to realize that while his heart lay with his scientific research, it was going to take more than science to free his people. Seeing the way the students in his classes responded, he began to think that focusing on education might have more of an immediate impact.

There was another famous African-American man working in the field of education—Booker T. Washington. Born a slave in Virginia in 1856 and freed by the Emancipation Proclamation in 1863, Washington taught himself to read and eventually worked his way through school at Hampton Institute in Virginia. Hampton was one of several schools for former slaves founded after the Civil War. It was set up so that African Americans could work and study at the same time. By the time he was twenty, Washington was a teacher at Hampton.

Washington went on to build the world-famous Tuskegee Institute in Alabama. There he emphasized training in the skilled trades over academic learning. Washington believed that African Americans must earn their place in society through hard work and financial success. Further, he thought that this financial success could only come to the majority of African Americans through skilled and unskilled labor. He put no particular value on higher education for the African Americans of his generation. Because his policies generally did not

Booker T. Washington. *(Library of Congress)*

question the established social order, Washington quickly became a popular and important figure for blacks and whites alike.

Du Bois had been a first-year instructor at Wilberforce in 1895 when Washington gave the famous speech that came to be known as the "Atlanta Compromise." This was the speech that vaulted Washington into the pantheon of important political figures.

Washington had been invited to speak at the Atlanta Cotton Exposition, which was to bring together Southern businessmen with Northern industrialists. Washington had steadily gained prestige as a spokesman for the

African-American population of the United States and had probably been invited to speak, at least in part, to show that the South had solved its racial problems.

Washington wanted his speech to give African Americans hope in the difficult days of increased lynchings and decreased freedoms, but he also didn't want to say anything that might cause the white majority to impose further restrictions. One famous line of his speech— "In all things that are purely social we can be as separate as the fingers, yet one as the hand in all things essential to mutual progress"—established that he was not in favor of disbanding segregation.

Washington's speech also outlined his belief that African Americans had to earn their rights: "The wisest among my race understand that the agitation of questions of social equality is the extremest folly, and that progress in the enjoyment of all the privileges that will come to us must be the result of severe and constant struggle, rather than of artificial forcing."

Washington's speech earned a ripple of approval throughout the United States. It was just what the people in power wanted to hear: the African-American problem was on its way to being solved. They congratulated themselves on supporting a black man of such obvious good sense as Booker T. Washington.

In the decade following his Atlanta Compromise speech, Washington's political power increased. Political appointments for African Americans were routed through Tuskegee for Washington's approval. In almost all issues related to blacks in the United States, government and business leaders consulted Washington.

Du Bois was unhappy with Washington and the message he sent. Du Bois believed that all men should have equal civil rights immediately—rights that were already guaranteed to them. The first step should be tearing down the laws allowing forced segregation. Du Bois called Washington and his advisors the Tuskegee Machine. He was frustrated that, as he saw it, "this Tuskegee Machine was not solely the idea and activity of black folk at Tuskegee. It was largely encouraged and given financial aid through certain white groups and individuals in the North." Du Bois believed this only furthered the economic exploitation of African Americans.

Perhaps more than anything else, Du Bois hated how the Tuskegee Machine smothered any dissenting voices. A black man who hoped to make a name for himself in the United States at the turn of the twentieth century had better be on the Tuskegee Machine's good side. The only way to be sure of that support was to not disagree with Booker T. Washington.

As well as influencing political appointments, Washington seemed to have considerable power over African-American-owned newspapers and other periodicals. Du Bois charged in a newspaper article that many of these newspapers were being supported financially by Washington so they would maintain a favorable tone toward Tuskegee.

More than fifty years later, as Du Bois admitted, the

Tuskegee model would be the norm: "These methods have become common enough in our day for all sorts of purposes: the distribution of advertising and favors, the sending out of special correspondence, veiled and open attacks upon recalcitrants, the narrowing of opportunities for employment and promotion." But at the turn of the century, Tuskegee represented just another form of oppression—all the more galling to Du Bois because it was run by African Americans.

Other black leaders shared Du Bois's concerns. Monroe Trotter, editor of the *Boston Guardian,* repeatedly attacked Washington's positions in his editorials. Trotter had also graduated with honors from Harvard in 1895. Together with George Forbes, he founded the *Guardian* in 1901. Trotter saw himself as a new abolitionist, fighting for black rights as the abolitionists had fought to end slavery before the Civil War. Trotter's disgust with Washington's conciliatory policies was well documented in the *Guardian.*

Monroe Trotter. *(Library of Congress)*

In contrast to Washington, Du Bois advocated a more aggressive pursuit of equality, mainly through education. Because he understood that not every black American could afford to or wanted to go to college, Du Bois came to advocate something he called the "talented tenth." According to Du Bois, the top ten percent of the African- American population, the best and the brightest, should go to college and take positions as leaders.

This concept of the talented tenth alarmed some people. They thought Du Bois was advocating a class of elites. But Du Bois believed that this talented tenth would serve as beacons to the rest. Du Bois reasoned that African Americans would always be subjected to white leadership if they didn't have members of their own race that were able to lead. The talented tenth were to be those leaders.

Du Bois said later of the differences between his talented tenth concept and Washington's beliefs, "These two theories of Negro progress were not absolutely contradictory." Du Bois saw the benefit of trade school and Washington was not totally opposed to universities—he sent his own children to college. However, they did have a basic difference of opinion that set the stage for more serious conflicts to come.

In the summer of 1903, Booker T. Washington traveled to Boston to speak at an African-American church. The meeting was contentious from the start, but the real trouble started when Monroe Trotter asked Washington several questions about education and voting. The questions upset the pro-Washington attendees at the meeting, and soon the event turned into what the newspapers called the Boston Riot—though the Boston Scuffle might have been a better description.

The various factions present began shouting and there was shoving in the aisles. The police soon arrived to restore the peace. Fresh outbursts occurred when it was discovered that cayenne pepper had been sprinkled on the podium, causing the next speaker to sneeze violently. Fistfights broke out and women swatted adversaries with their purses. Trotter jumped up and down on a pew yelling questions to Washington, who sat motionless on the platform watching the melee in front of him.

Finally, Trotter was hauled away by the police, the crowd quieted, and Washington finished his speech. Trotter was charged with disorderly conduct and served thirty days in jail. Du Bois had nothing to do with the incident, but he was upset that Trotter ended up in jail. Du Bois said, "I did not always agree with Trotter then or later. But he was an honest, brilliant, unselfish man, and to treat as a crime that which was at worst mistaken judgment was an outrage."

After the dust had settled in Boston, Washington accused Du Bois of being behind the attacks. President Bumstead and the trustees at Atlanta University became alarmed by the charges. Du Bois wrote a letter to them in which he accounted for his activities prior to the Boston uproar to prove that he had not been involved. The board was satisfied with his explanation except for one sentence in the last paragraph of the letter. Du Bois could not keep himself from adding, "As between Trotter and Mr. Washington, I unhesitatingly believe Mr. Trotter to be far nearer the right." Du Bois had chosen his side. He was now generally associated with those who demanded complete and immediate equality for African Americans—and who stood in opposition to Booker T. Washington and Tuskegee.

In 1903, Du Bois published what would be his most successful book. *The Souls of Black Folk* was a collection of essays, including one titled "Of Mr. Booker T. Washington and Others." In this essay Du Bois outlined Washington's views and problems he saw with them. Although he had long disagreed with Washington, Du

A page from Du Bois's manuscript of *The Souls of Black Folk*. *(Special Collections and Archives, W.E.B. Du Bois Library, University of Massachusetts Amherst)*

Bois was now, for the first time, publicly splitting with the powerful leader. By openly criticizing Washington's policy of appeasement, Du Bois departed the middle ground he had long occupied. Du Bois said later that this book signaled the end of a period of his life.

*The Souls of Black Folk* was received with open arms by most readers. Its poignancy and the clarity of its words moved people of all races and backgrounds. Letters poured in from across the country, thanking Du Bois profusely for giving voice to the feelings they too had struggled with. It was in this book that Du Bois first explored something he called a double consciousness: being aware of being black and being an American, and feeling torn between those two identities. For the first time, readers could imagine what it might be like to experience the horrors and effects of racism.

Some reviewers and newspapers chose to ignore Du Bois's book completely. Others dismissed his claims, saying that black people were happy. Du Bois's experience writing and publishing the book was cataclysmic. From 1903 on, he became a more vocal and visible activist, speaking out in favor of civil rights. For him, it was obvious: blacks should be able to vote, have equal justice under the law, attend good schools, and exercise the freedoms available to every American. He still believed in voluntary segregation, especially as it regarded African-American-owned businesses, but he was well on the road to being a political agitator as well as a scholar.

# Five

# The NAACP

Du Bois's conflict with Booker T. Washington put him in a perilous position within the African-American community. He could either find enough backers to mount a challenge to Washington's dominance, or he could be abandoned and ignored. Luckily for Du Bois, he was not the only person who felt the time had come for direct action.

In the spring of 1905, Du Bois called a meeting of a few of his supporters to ask them to help him form a social action committee. When he was twenty-five, Du Bois had vowed to change the world. Now he realized scholarship was not the only way to do so. With the committee's support Du Bois planned a conference that was held near Buffalo, New York, during the week of July 9, 1905. The men met in a small hotel on the Canadian side of Niagara Falls.

A group picture from the first meeting of the Niagara Movement in July 1905. Du Bois is in the center with the light-colored hat. *(Special Collections and Archives, W.E.B. Du Bois Library, University of Massachusetts Amherst)*

Out of that conference came a group which became known as the Niagara Movement. Made up of citizens and leaders who were willing to challenge Washington and to speak out, they took a tough stance, demanding equal voting and civil rights for all people. The organization's "Declaration of Principles," written by Du Bois and Monroe Trotter, called for:

1. Freedom of speech and criticism.
2. An unfettered and unsubsidized press.
3. Manhood suffrage.
4. The abolition of all caste distinctions based simply on race and color.
5. The recognition of the principle of human brotherhood as a practical present creed.
6. The recognition of the highest and best human training as the monopoly of no class or race.
7. A belief in the dignity of labor.
8. United effort to realize these ideals under wise and courageous leadership.

The declaration might seem reasonable now, but in 1905, African Americans had none of these rights and privileges in the South, and few of them in the North. Washington supporters, or Bookerites as they were sometimes called, were angry at Du Bois and the others because Washington had counseled blacks to abandon or delay asking for these rights. The Niagara Declaration was a slap in the face to Washington, who preached accommodation to whites at almost any cost.

The Niagara Movement weathered the criticism and met again in 1906 in West Virginia. At this meeting they drafted resolutions dedicating their lives, honor, and property to the freeing of their people. They rejected violence in any form, but supported other methods to agitate for civil rights.

The uproar over the Niagara Movement still simmered in September 1906 when events took a violent turn in Atlanta. For several months, the atmosphere in that city had been tense. A local political campaign had centered on suppressing black voting rights and produced hysterical speeches by segregationists as well as newspaper articles stirring up racist sentiments. The last straw came when newspapers published unsubstantiated accounts of African-American men assaulting white women.

It was a deep-seated hatred and fear that boiled over in the streets of Atlanta on the evening of September 22, 1906. A white mob, 10,000 strong, roamed through the city. They beat every black person they could find. African-American-owned businesses were destroyed and their proprietors beaten. The mobs targeted black employees at the train station and post office, and those who worked in white-owned businesses. They grabbed blacks off passing trolleys. By dawn, ten blacks and two whites were dead. Several hundred more people were injured.

Du Bois was away in Alabama when the riot occurred. He hurried home, fearing that his wife and six-year-old daughter, Yolande, were in danger. On the way home on the train, he wrote a long poem called "A Litany at Atlanta," which reflected his despair about the violence.

Yolande and Nina were fine, but Du Bois was boiling

with rage. He later wrote, "I bought a Winchester double-barreled shotgun and two dozen rounds of shells filled with buckshot. If a white mob had stepped on the campus where I lived, I would without hesitation have sprayed their guts over the grass." The mob did not come, but the scholarly Du Bois had more fuel for his activism.

Du Bois pursued the establishment of an African-American-owned magazine or paper that would support activists. With few exceptions, the existing publications backed Washington's theme of conciliation with whites. First, Du Bois started a paper called *The Moon*. He gave that up after a year and started a monthly magazine called *Horizon*. It became the official publication of the Niagara Movement.

The Niagara Movement continued to meet and agitate for black voting rights, but was always hampered by a lack of money. The Niagara Movement's greatest achievement may have been that its very existence gave hope to black Americans.

In 1909, another organization rose to take the Niagara Movement's place. It began as a response to yet another terrible race riot, which occurred in Springfield, Illinois, on August 14, 1908. A young African-American man was accused of raping the white wife of a street railway worker. The alleged crime was the stated cause for the riot, but the explosive violence had other, deeper causes as well.

The number of African Americans in the Springfield area had grown steadily as blacks moved northward to find better economic conditions. Many of the new arrivals became quite successful working in the mines and in rail transportation. This prosperity did not go unnoticed among the white residents of the area, and the resulting resentment fueled the Springfield riot.

As tensions heightened in Springfield, the sheriff tried to move the accused rapist out of town, along with another black man accused of murdering a white man. The sheriff had the town's fire trucks race up and down the streets to create a distraction while he removed the prisoners by car to safety. When a gathering mob realized they had been tricked, they surged on to damage and destroy anything in their path. Eventually, they lynched two men. One was a barber who had tried to

During the riots, the Illinois state militia camped on the statehouse lawn in Springfield. *(Library of Congress)*

protect his property and the other was an eighty-year-old man who was married to a white woman. He was dragged from his home and pounded to death with bricks.

The state militia was called out, but there would be two days of destruction before the riot was over. Four whites were killed and hundreds of both races were injured. Whole blocks had been reduced to smoking ruins.

One of the things that set this race riot apart was that it happened in the North, in the land of Lincoln. Abraham Lincoln, the president who had issued the Emancipation Proclamation, was buried in Springfield, and the town had already begun preparations to celebrate his one-hundredth birthday. The Springfield riot brought home the fact that extreme violence against African Americans was not confined to the South.

In 1900, statistics show that an average of $15.41 a year was spent on educating a white child in America, while only $1.50 was spent to educate an African-American child. There were separate waiting rooms at train stations and separate railway cars. Blacks had to sit in the back of theaters, many churches, and busses. There were separate drinking fountains in public places, and many businesses had separate entrances. In some cases, when blacks were barred from entering or patronizing a whites-only establishment, there simply was no alternative for them nearby—no store, no hotel, no public bathroom that would allow a black person to enter. The effect was a radical segregation and the continued abuse of African Americans.

In reaction to the riot, a group of liberal white leaders formed a political action committee in New York City, and invited Du Bois to join them. The group planned a conference, which began on May 31, 1909. It brought together a number of people from all backgrounds and perspectives. As Du Bois remembered, "This conference contained four groups: scientists who knew the race problem; philanthropists willing to help worthy causes; social workers ready to take up a new task of abolition; and Negroes ready to join a new crusade for their emancipation."

The organization was first called the National Negro Committee, and the following year was formally named the National Association for the Advancement of Colored People. It was usually referred to as the NAACP. At first, its leaders were white, but many prominent African Americans soon joined the group. Few of Washington's supporters were among them.

The purpose of the NAACP was to work against discrimination and segregation using legal action and education as their main weapons. The national organization soon expanded to include many local groups or chapters, which would eventually handle local problems themselves while reporting back to the national office.

The founding of the NAACP was one of the first major public steps taken in an effort to combat the racism and prejudice rampant in the country. Though the organizers knew they were placing themselves in danger by vowing to stand up for the rights and protections promised to African Americans by law, they could not stand by and allow the violence to continue. People white and black offered financial backing to the fledgling group, and forty-one-year-old W. E. B. Du Bois—though it meant abandoning his career as a scientist—took his place among those willing to risk their lives for freedom.

Du Bois was the only black member of the board of

Letter from NAACP secretary Francis Blascoer offering Du Bois the position of director of publicity and research. *(Special Collections and Archives, W.E.B. Du Bois Library, University of Massachusetts Amherst)*

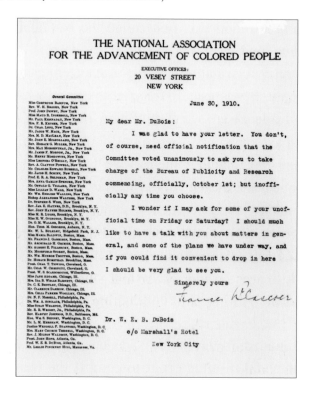

New York City was a bustling and modern city at the turn of the century. *(Library of Congress)*

directors and was also appointed as director of publicity and research. In August 1910, he left Atlanta University and moved to New York City. This move was both geographic and metaphoric. Du Bois was making a transition from scholar to activist. He continued his association with the university for several more years as he helped with the Atlanta studies, but his focus was changing.

Du Bois's title of director of publicity and research implied that he would continue his research, but in reality there was no money for that. His most important job became editing and publishing *The Crisis*, the NAACP's magazine. After much discussion among the NAACP board of directors, it was decided that the new magazine could reflect Du Bois's editorial opinions rather than a more general statement of the purpose of the association. Though Du Bois and the NAACP as a group shared many of the same philosophies and approaches, Du Bois was anxious that he be allowed to write freely in what he thought of as his magazine. He did not want to be just the mouthpiece of the organization.

Du Bois intended *The Crisis* to serve several purposes. It would report on events in the United States and around the world that had to do with interracial relations. In his first editorial, Du Bois explained that the magazine would also review books, articles, and expressions of opinion from the white and black press. *The Crisis* would also contain a few short articles. In general, as Du Bois put it, "The object of this publication is to set forth those facts and arguments which show the danger of race prejudice, particularly as manifested toward colored people. It takes its name from the fact that the editors believe that this is a critical time in the history of the advancement of men."

The first issue of the magazine was published in November 1910. Within three years the circulation grew from 1,000 copies a month to 30,000. Perhaps its greatest significance for African Americans was confirming that they were being treated badly by whites and offering hope that this treatment might cease. The NAACP did not demand special rights for African Americans, but wanted equal rights, and with those rights an equal chance to succeed in America. Du Bois supported the association in this aim and searched for aggressive ways

to make this happen.

The association's attitude toward Booker T. Washington and how it should be expressed was a complicated issue. Washington was the most prominent and well-liked African American of the time— by blacks and whites alike. Yet in the fall of 1910, Washington was in Europe giving speeches saying that the race issue in the United States was on its way to

The first issue of *The Crisis*, published in November 1910.

being solved. Du Bois and the NAACP board disagreed strongly.

Du Bois wrote that while Washington was a distinguished American and welcome to his opinion, Du Bois did not agree with his conclusions. He pointed to the fact that news of lynchings and other crimes against blacks were reported daily. In August 1910 alone, there were newspaper reports of the killing of at least twenty African Americans in the southern United States. In Florida, four black men were lynched for one alleged murder. In Palestine, Texas, it was reported that at least fifteen and maybe as many as twenty African Americans were hunted down and killed by a mob on the night of July 31. The local sheriff reported that a misunderstanding over a promissory note had apparently caused the trouble.

During these years, Du Bois traveled and spoke often. His reputation as a speaker and scholar grew. He was asked to speak at the Universal Races Congress in London in 1911. It was the first international meeting of scientists devoted to social reform and racial equality. That Du Bois was asked to address the congress was a lift to the prestige of the NAACP.

Still, it seemed that for every achievement there was a setback. In the southern United States, an insect called the boll weevil, which destroyed cotton, had come from Mexico. It combined with a series of droughts and floods to devastate the cotton industry, which meant that hundreds of thousands of blacks were put out of work. They migrated in great streams to the Northern industrial cities, where many of them ended up in segregated poor neighborhoods called ghettos.

Discrimination in the Northern states had always been present, but there had generally been more tolerance and certainly less violence than in the South. This changed with the great influx of blacks into the Northern cities. Whites saw the migrants as a threat to their jobs and communities. In response to this perceived threat, some trades refused to admit African Americans, Jim Crow laws continued to spread, and there was the ever-present threat of violence. The Northern courts often followed their Southern counterparts' ways, failing repeatedly to provide fair trials for African-American defendants. Every means possible was used to keep the newly arrived blacks from gaining economic or political power. Du Bois, like many others, despaired at the way African Americans were being treated.

In 1911, Du Bois joined the Socialist Party. Ever since he had first read Marx at Harvard and then studied him further while in Germany, Du Bois had been a proponent of socialist thinking. He admired the way socialism promised to help the underprivileged—regardless of race.

Socialism was attractive to Du Bois because, as an economic system, it advocates that workers share ownership of the means of production. For example, in a socialist system, factory workers would own and run the factory where they worked rather than answering to a single owner or board of directors. The workers would then share equally in the factory profits according to each one's needs. A man with five children would receive a higher percentage of the profit than a man who was not married and had no children, because the man with five children had a greater need. Socialists also advocated more government control and regulation of public utilities, transportation, and other industries providing services for the common good—such as healthcare.

Socialist ideas have existed for centuries but came to the forefront during the European Industrial Revolution in the early to mid-1800s. At the time, there were few laws regulating the workplace and most people worked

long hours for very little pay—often in highly dangerous conditions. The Industrial Revolution also created
tremendous disparity between the rich and the poor.
Socialism offered the promise of better working conditions and treatment. Many of the people who were a part
of the growing Progressive movement in America came
to identify themselves as Socialists or Communists (a
related philosophy), because both of these systems promised equality without regard for race, religion, or creed.

Since Du Bois's time working in the Seventh Ward of
Philadelphia, the Progressive movement had continued
to grow and develop. By the early twentieth century, it
was a loose affiliation of activists working to help
various underserved populations. In 1912, when former
president Theodore Roosevelt decided to contest Republican president William Howard Taft's bid for reelection, he formed the Progressive Party in order to do so.
Roosevelt ran on a platform that promised many social
reforms, including offering the vote to women. He was
able to gain the support of many prominent reformers,
including Jane Addams of Hull House, who also worked
for the NAACP.

Du Bois was among those who supported the Democratic contender, the former governor of New Jersey
Woodrow Wilson. Du Bois resigned from the Socialist
Party in 1912 to support Wilson, who had indicated to
leaders of the NAACP and others that he would protect
the interests of African Americans and veto any legislation that was unfavorable to blacks.

Du Bois *(far right)* at work in the offices of *The Crisis. (Library of Congress)*

Du Bois had been skeptical about Wilson's promises but finally endorsed the candidate in *The Crisis* in August 1912. However, it was soon apparent that Wilson was unwilling or unable to act on his promises. As Wilson watched from the White House, Republican African-American officeholders in the South were replaced with white Democrats. When Wilson did venture to nominate African Americans for federal job appointments, he encountered fierce opposition from the Senate and threats to stall his legislative program. Wilson considered his plans for economic reform to be the most important job before him. He was willing to make deals and turn the other way when it came to race relations in order to gain support for his legislative plans.

Subsequently, several pieces of legislation were introduced in the U.S. Congress and in numerous states that proposed to limit freedoms for African Americans more than ever before. They included bills advocating Jim Crow cars on trains in Washington, D.C., the exclusion of blacks from commissions in the army and navy, and a ban on interracial marriage. Most of the bills never passed, but under Wilson's watch, the federal government itself was segregated. African-American employees were to have separate work stations, dining areas, and bathrooms.

This caused an outcry among NAACP leaders, and even Booker T. Washington voiced disapproval. Oswald Garrison Villard, a white newspaper publisher, philanthropist, and NAACP board member, wrote letters to Wilson, arranged meetings with Wilson's staff, and met with the president himself to protest this further degradation.

Wilson refused to reverse the policies. Apparently, he had told his cabinet members to handle any problems with African-American employees in a way that would cause the least trouble. He later defended the resulting segregation as being in the best interest of blacks as well as whites. President Wilson saw himself as an enlightened Southerner who wanted fairness for all men and women, but privately thought that African Americans would progress much faster if they worked with members of their own race.

The coming of World War I distracted much of America's attention and, without much fanfare, many of the segregationist policies were at least partially reversed by the end of 1914. The war, however, would bring new problems.

Booker T. Washington died in 1915, and with him died much of the division within the African-American community. There would continue to be differences of opinion about strategy in the struggle for freedom, but Washington's accommodationist ideas had generally fallen out of favor. The Civil War was fifty years in the past and America was a changed place. What became known as the Gilded Age was a time of tremendous economic and industrial growth. It also saw a great increase in the number of poor people and brought new attention to their plight. Disadvantaged people everywhere needed change.

W. E. B. Du Bois was now the most well-known black leader in America, and he used *The Crisis* to rally African Americans to demand change. One of his first challenges would be the discriminatory policies revealed by World War I.

# Six

# Gathering Storm

World War I began in 1914 as a response to the assassination of Austrian Archduke Francis Ferdinand by a Serbian loyalist. The war was soon joined by Russia, France, and Britain against Germany, Austria-Hungary, and Turkey. Initially, most Americans saw it as a European conflict and wanted to stay neutral. But when German U-boats (submarines) sank the passenger ship *Lusitania* in 1915, 123 Americans were among the 1,195 killed. President Wilson was reelected in 1916 on the slogan "he kept us out of war," but public opinion was already running against Germany. When Wilson's efforts to mediate between the warring factions failed, and Germany promised to continue submarine attacks, America began to prepare to send troops across the ocean.

Du Bois had been bitterly disappointed by Wilson's failure to carry through on promises to support African-American causes and by the segregation of the United States government. Feeling abandoned by the Democratic Party, he had urged African Americans to support the Socialist presidential candidate in the 1916 election. Socialism held out the promise of equality Du Bois did not see forthcoming from the federal government or the capitalist system. But Wilson won the election, and, in 1917, Congress declared war on Germany. The role black soldiers would play suddenly became a major issue.

African Americans had fought in the armed forces, often with distinction, since the Civil War. By the time World War I began, there were four all-black regiments in the army, each led by white commanding officers. Just days after Congress declared war, so many African Americans volunteered for duty the army had to turn them away—the four regiments reserved for them were full.

In May of 1917, one month after declaring war, Congress passed the Selective Service Act, which provided for drafting troops to increase the size of the armed forces. In an interesting example of reverse discrimination, African Americans were much less likely to be rejected by (all-white) draft boards than white draftees were. Black men were welcomed into the army in large numbers—though they were generally trained and housed separately. And though black soldiers in the army were eligible for most positions, they were much more likely to be assigned to menial jobs.

This poster from World War I shows African-American soldiers bravely fighting Germans with an image of Lincoln overhead. This romantic portrayal of warfare encouraged many African Americans to join the military, but the reality of their conditions and treatment was far from glorious. *(Library of Congress)*

The influx of black soldiers to the army (blacks were not allowed to join the Marines and could obtain only menial positions in the Coast Guard or the Navy) created a problem inasmuch as there were no African-American officers to train the black troops. This could have been dealt with by having white training officers, but the NAACP fought this. They wanted African Americans trained as commissioned officers to command and train black soldiers. Du Bois and other leaders would have preferred to have total integration but agreed to the separate training as the best of the poor alternatives. They felt forced to agree to segregation in order to obtain some degree of fairness for the black draftees.

As a result of the popular outcry led by the NAACP, several hundred black officers received commissions and assumed command of black units. Though they still faced discrimination and inferior conditions, having black officers was seen as a big step forward. In addition, the war economy was creating new jobs—for blacks as well as whites. In 1918, Du Bois wrote an editorial in *The Crisis* entitled "Close Ranks." In it he explained that, in his view, victory in the war was the most important objective for all Americans, black or white: "Let us, while this war lasts, forget our special grievances and close ranks shoulder to shoulder with our fellow citizens and the allied nations that are fighting for democracy. We make no ordinary sacrifice, but we make it gladly and willingly with our eyes lifted to the hills."

Du Bois's support for the war was complicated, as he later wrote, "I did not believe in war, but I thought that in a fight with America against militarism and for democracy we would be fighting for the emancipation of the Negro race." Despite having some evidence to the contrary, Du Bois still clung to the belief that discrimination could be triumphed over by education. When white people realized that black soldiers fought bravely and gave their lives the same way white soldiers did, he sincerely believed they would change their minds about seeing blacks as inferior.

Other black leaders did not necessarily support Du Bois's views. They felt he was advocating segregation, which they could not do. Du Bois remained a believer in voluntary segregation, but the segregation of the armed forces wasn't voluntary. Still, Du Bois was willing to accept it as a temporary solution, which some people saw as the kind of conciliatory policy Booker T. Washington had been criticized for just a few years before. Du Bois tried to explain that he hoped the gains would outweigh the sacrifices, but his words rang false for some listeners. And the real trouble was yet to come.

World War I officially ended in the fall of 1918. Once it was over, the NAACP sent Du Bois to Europe to investigate the treatment of black soldiers. He found that racism was rampant. Though Europeans tended to discriminate less than Americans, Du Bois discovered that American racism had infected their European counterparts. The French government had issued directives to its military not to get too friendly with black soldiers because it would upset the Americans. Du Bois reported his findings in a scathing May 1919 editorial in *The Crisis*. He was furious that 100,000 African Americans could risk their lives alongside white soldiers and yet still be treated like second-class citizens.

After his investigation, Du Bois stayed in Paris, France, to convene a Pan-African Congress in February 1919. He modeled it on the first such conference, which had been organized by Henry Sylvester Williams and attended by Du Bois in 1900. The stated purpose of the 1919 conference was to free African nations from colonial rule, but American blacks as well as blacks who lived in Africa or the West Indies were intended to be part of the movement. For Du Bois, the liberation of black people all over the world was as important as the liberation of black people in the United States.

In the early twentieth century, much of the continent

Map of colonial Africa in the early twentieth century.

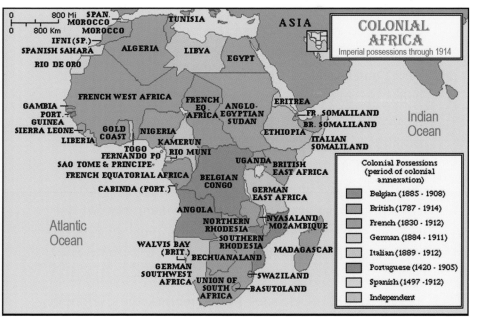

The Second Pan-African Congress, 1921. Du Bois is seated second from the right. *(Special Collections and Archives, W.E.B. Du Bois Library, University of Massachusetts Amherst)*

of Africa was under the control of various European countries. Those colonizing powers had moved into Africa in order to obtain its rich natural resources. Though colonialists argued that they helped their colonies by sharing with them advances in technology, education, science, and infrastructure, Du Bois and others saw colonizers as oppressive and exploitative. The Pan-Africa movement wanted to bring independence to colonized countries.

Because Pan-Africanism threatened the economic stability of the colonizing countries, it was not a popular movement in many parts of Europe and America. Many businesses and governments benefited from African colonies and had no desire to abandon them. But Du Bois and his supporters were determined to draw attention to the abuses of colonialism.

Three Pan-African Congresses were held between 1919 and 1923. Delegates from America, the Caribbean nations, and Africa attended. A few representatives of colonial powers also attended. The conferences were, in keeping with their leader, serious, scholarly endeavors. They focused on designing and advocating programs to unite black Africa, but, as Du Bois admitted, they "were chiefly memorable for the excitement and opposition which they caused among the colonial imperialists."

The opposition to Pan-Africanism was considerable, and Du Bois complained that it was partly due to the press confusing his movement, probably on purpose, with Marcus Garvey's Black Nationalist movement, which was at its peak.

Marcus Garvey was born in Jamaica in 1887. He worked as a printer and journalist in several countries before forming the Universal Negro Improvement Association (UNIA) in Jamaica in 1914. He was greatly influenced by Booker T. Washington's writing. He came to the United States after the war and traveled throughout the country to

Marcus Garvey. *(Library of Congress)*

promote his ideas, becoming a powerful spokesman for black nationalism.

Black nationalism emphasized racial pride and unity, economic cooperation, identification with Africa, and an interest in racial history. Garvey, a charismatic speaker, soon had thousands of supporters. Frustrated by years of discrimination and defeat, they were drawn by his message of empowerment. Part of his success was also due to the timing of his crusade. Race relations in 1919 in the United States were explosive, and the environment was ripe for change.

When black soldiers returned home from fighting in Europe, they expected to encounter more job opportunities and increased freedoms from the country they had risked their lives to defend. African Americans who had benefited from the economic boom now had higher expectations about education and employment. But instead of opening up, society closed down and blacks found racism and discrimination even more vicious than before. A decade of migration northward had left large numbers of blacks in the big cities of the North. All of these social and demographic changes played a part in what became known as the "Red Summer" of 1919.

That summer, race riots raged in more than twenty cities across the United States, including Omaha, Tulsa, and Knoxville. In Washington, D.C., the rioting involved uniformed sailors and soldiers chasing and beating African-American men and women within sight of the U.S. Capitol. In Omaha the mob turned on its mayor when

he and other authorities tried to stop an attempted lynching. The mob then tried to lynch the mayor and he later died of his injuries.

The worst of the riots occurred in Chicago in late July. It started at a beach on Lake Michigan when a young black man in the water strayed into the area reserved for white swimmers. A crowd of white men began throwing rocks at him and the swimmer drowned. The rock throwers, though clearly identified to the police, were not arrested. This injustice was the spark that ignited more than a week's worth of violence in Chicago. Mobs both black and white roamed the city, inflicting tremendous damage. The police called to maintain order sometimes

*The Chicago Daily Tribune* from July 28, 1919, details the continuing violence from the summer's race riots.

sided with the white rioters, creating further chaos. The Chicago riots left twenty-three blacks and fifteen whites dead, and 537 more people wounded. Over one hundred families, mostly black, found themselves homeless because of property destruction.

There was one big difference between this riot and others in the past, and some African Americans saw it as a turning point. African Americans fought back against the mobs in Chicago. In some neighborhoods, they banded together to fend off white attackers. Some leaders wondered if this resistance might actually be a good thing. They speculated that if whites saw that blacks would not tolerate abuse, whites would adjust their views and accept integration.

During this summer the NAACP launched investigations into several of the riots across the country. The association itself was implicated in at least one of the riots. Rumors were circulating in Texas that the NAACP was inciting revolt and the NAACP secretary, John Shillady, was attacked. Shillady never completely recovered, and he resigned as secretary the next spring.

Attacks like the one on Shillady galvanized the public. Ninety thousand people had joined the NAACP by 1920. Just a decade old, the organization had quickly become a major player in American society and politics. It was also highly controversial. The NAACP board was divided about whether to hold the 1920 national conference in Atlanta, as planned, or to move it to a Northern city. There was much concern that having the conference in Atlanta might cause a riot, and concern that moving the conference might imply fear or defeat. In the end, determination to meet in the deep South and a cordial invitation from the mayor of Atlanta brought dissenters around. The conference went off without any violence.

Marcus Garvey's speeches about black pride and the importance of activism resonated with people tired of feeling inferior or shunted aside, particularly members of the working class. Garvey was a proponent of Pan-Africanism, but he took the idea a step further, advocating a back-to-Africa movement. According to Garvey, people of African descent would never be able to achieve equality in the United States. They would be better off returning to the land of their ancestors and making a new society there. Within a few years, Garvey had attracted thousands of followers, planned the Black Star steamship line, and started the highly influential *Negro World* newspaper.

Du Bois initially admired Garvey, calling him "an extraordinary leader of men." Though he did not always agree with Garvey, he understood why people flocked to him. Garvey offered hope, however impractical that hope might be, to a people beaten down by constant conflict. Du Bois and the NAACP would accomplish more for black rights in the long run, but their tactics could not compare to the thrill of walking behind Marcus Garvey in a parade 50,000 people strong. Legal challenges and editorials—no matter how scorching— were just not as invigorating. Still, Du Bois and many others considered a mass exodus by African Americans to Africa to be an impossible and impractical approach.

In 1922, Garvey made a decision that lost him most of his support in the black community. He asked the Ku Klux Klan, a white supremacist organization, for help with his back-to-Africa movement. Though he did not support the violence perpetrated by the Klan, Garvey thought the group could help his cause. He rejected the integrationist approach favored by the NAACP, effectively severing his ties with that part of the movement. Du Bois denounced Garvey angrily in the pages of *The Crisis* and in speeches across the country. Most of Garvey's supporters broke ranks and joined the NAACP, isolating the increasingly volatile leader. Three years later, Garvey would be sent to federal prison for mail fraud. In 1927, he was pardoned by President Coolidge and deported to Jamaica. Once removed from the American scene, his influence was considerably diminished and the back-to-Africa movement slowed almost to a halt.

While Du Bois and others were disappointed that Garvey would chose the Klan over the NAACP, the biggest problem he posed had to do with public relations. His back-to-Africa movement and Du Bois's Pan-Africanism were often paired in the press and therefore in people's minds. Pan-Africanism suffered as a result.

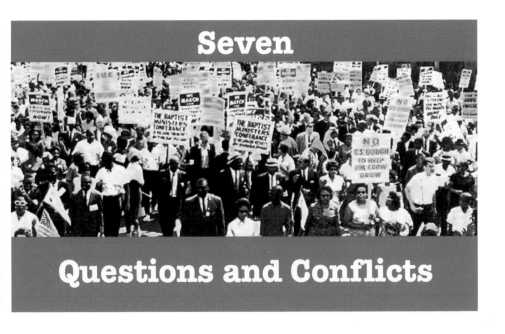

# Seven

# Questions and Conflicts

Du Bois's conflict with Garvey highlighted the fact that what was becoming the civil rights movement was born in fits and starts and changed along the way.

Du Bois was among those people who looked to the American Socialist Party for inspiration. Since joining the party in 1911, Du Bois had hoped that socialism's tenants of equality would help achieve racial parity. But he eventually became disappointed with what he saw as the party's inattention to race issues.

In 1926, Du Bois made a trip to Russia to see how the new Communist government there was working. Communists, who advocated for radical change as compared to the evolutionary change Socialists favored, had seized control in a 1917 revolution, hoping to end the tyrannous rule of the czars and bring the people out of economic, social, and political oppression. Once in power, the Communists implemented a Socialist government designed to redistribute the wealth of the land and provide food, education, and jobs for everyone.

Du Bois's tour of Russia left him impressed by the new government. "Never before had I seen so many among a suppressed mass of poor, working people—people as ignorant, poor, superstitious and cowed as my own American Negroes—so lifted in hope and starry-eyed with new determination," he wrote. It also confirmed Du Bois's suspicions that merely ensuring African Americans had the right to vote was not going to solve their work and wage problems, abolish illiteracy, or decrease sickness and crime—not unless it was supplemented by economic change. Du Bois announced, "I believe in the dictum of Karl Marx, that the economic foundation of a nation is widely decisive for its politics, its art and its culture."

Du Bois's trip to Russia marked a turning point in some of his thinking. Afterward, he focused less and less on sociology and scientific investigation as the road to social reform for African Americans, and more on economic revolution as the answer. Eventually his plan for reform would include any people confined within a class system, whether or not they were black.

After his trip to Russia, Du Bois saw the United States through new eyes. He was even more aware of the class differences that stratified American society, and he continued to be disappointed that more activists were not addressing economic issues. From his perspective, Americans were too caught up in the excitement of the economic boom of the 1920s to realize how it was affecting those at the bottom of society. Du Bois's vision of a talented tenth, an educated and prosperous group who would lead other African Americans to freedom, seemed as distant as ever. Society was changing, but not the way Du Bois had hoped.

What came to be known as the Harlem Renaissance began in New York when thousands of Southern blacks moved north in search of better jobs and better lives. A vibrant community of artists and writers grew in Harlem, creating a stimulating cultural and social environment. Jazz music thrilled black and white nightclub patrons alike. The publishing industry thrived as writers, including Langston Hughes, Zora Neale Hurston, Countee Cullen, and Jean Toomer, brought the experiences of black Americans to life as never before. A popular book by Alain Locke called *The New Negro: An Interpretation* summarized the way the lives of African Americans were changing. The Harlem Renaissance brought black pride, education, and a new spirit of optimism.

Du Bois had a complicated relationship with the Harlem Renaissance. While he was happy to see black artists doing well and selling their work to people on both sides of the color line, he disapproved of any literature that in any way denigrated African Americans. In his view, propaganda was preferable to art. He became angry when he read books by black writers that featured

Harlem Renaissance painter William Johnson was famous for his depictions of everyday African-American life. This painting, called *Street Life, Harlem,* was made in the 1930s. *(Library of Congress)*

black characters that were "slow" or spoke in dialect. He felt black writers had a responsibility to portray their race in a positive light. But most writers disagreed and resented Du Bois's criticism. They wanted to be free to express their ideas the way they wanted, not restricted to making only political art.

*Dark Princess,* a novel published in 1928, was Du Bois's own contribution to the Harlem Renaissance. In accordance with his philosophy of writing, the book is a political commentary first and foremost. The plot revolves around a group made up of minorities from around the world who unite in order to overcome colonialism and racism. Some critics disparaged the work as heavy-handed and overly political, while others appreciated Du Bois's heartfelt politics.

Another literary figure became a part of the Du Bois family when the well-known poet Countee Cullen married Yolande Du Bois in 1928. The wedding was held at

Countee Cullen (*front center*) married Yolande Du Bois in an elaborate celebration. Du Bois and Nina are pictured to the right of Cullen. Writers Langston Hughes and Arna Bontemps (*back row, center*) were ushers in the ceremony. *(Special Collections and Archives, W.E.B. Du Bois Library, University of Massachusetts Amherst)*

the Salem Methodist Episcopal Church in Harlem. More than 3,000 people watched the ceremony while live canaries sang from ornate cages in the church. The marriage would not succeed, and the couple divorced in 1930.

In June of 1929, Du Bois spoke at the twentieth anniversary meeting of the NAACP. There, he was optimistic about the new sense of black solidarity on the rise across the nation. Du Bois pointed out the numerous successes of the previous two decades, including the way the NAACP had demanded the right to vote for blacks and used the courts to fight discrimination in every way they could. Du Bois's message was much the same as it had been when the NAACP was founded, but now more African Americans were ready to stand up for the rights they had long been denied. They were willing to join him in the fight for freedom.

This great surge of optimism was dealt a heavy blow that very same year when the stock market crash of October 1929 began the Great Depression. The decade before had been a prosperous one for many people, but there had also been warning signs of trouble to come. When it came, it was catastrophic. Within three years, nearly one-third of Americans would be out of work. The Depression caused thousands of banks to close, taking with them people's life savings. Businesses were forced to shut their doors and poverty ravaged the nation.

Among those hardest hit by the Depression were those people already on the edges of society—many of

A group photograph from the twentieth annual meeting of the NAACP in 1929.
*(Library of Congress)*

whom were black. Finding work had long been difficult for African Americans; now it became nearly impossible. Unemployment rates reached as high as fifty percent in some industries, and those African Americans who had achieved middle-class status now found themselves poor and hungry. It would take a long time to recover from the worst economic crisis the world had ever known.

Du Bois and *The Crisis* were among those deeply affected by the Depression. Circulation dropped off sharply because few people had money for subscriptions. It was soon apparent to Du Bois that his publication would have to get financial support from the NAACP if it was to survive.

*The Crisis* had always been financially independent from the NAACP, and that had given Du Bois a certain freedom of expression. Over the years, some of his beliefs had begun to differ from the association's official stands on controversial issues. Du Bois feared that asking for financial support from the NAACP would restrict his freedom to write what he felt. One of their biggest differences of opinion was over segregation.

Du Bois wanted total freedom for all blacks in every aspect of society, but he had come to believe that complete desegregation was not going to happen anytime soon. With this in mind, he advocated organized economic cooperation among blacks: blacks should support black businesses and other black enterprises. Du Bois expressed again that black schools should be improved so children could get a decent education—even if they were segregated from whites. The NAACP, on the other hand, advocated for desegregation in all areas of society. Anything separate was inherently unequal.

The two sides had managed an uneasy truce for many years, but their differences could not be overlooked forever. After the Russian revolution of 1917, Du Bois authored numerous editorials in the pages of *The Crisis* that praised the new Communist government. His favorable comments about Marxism were not popular with many subscribers. Even his enthusiasm for Pan-Africanism was greeted with some dismay by the more conservative NAACP board, which felt he might be moving too fast.

The differences Du Bois had with his fellow board members might have been smoothed over were it not for the Depression. The board felt *The Crisis* must reflect the views of the NAACP more precisely if it was being financially supported by that organization. Du Bois entered a difficult period of his career as he tried to stay true to his beliefs yet honor the organization that had provided him a way to explain and advocate those beliefs.

The beginning of the end of Du Bois's career as editor of *The Crisis* came in 1931 when Walter White became executive secretary of the NAACP. White had been assistant secretary for over ten years, but his ascendancy to the executive position brought him into conflict with the always-opinionated Du Bois.

Walter White. *(Library of Congress)*

Du Bois later described White as charming and a tireless worker. But Du Bois objected to what he saw as the way White's own views dominated the NAACP: "He was absolutely self-centered and egotistical to the point that he was almost unconscious of it. He seemed really to believe that his personal interests and the interest of his race and organization were identical. This led to curious complications, because to obtain his objects he was often absolutely unscrupulous."

In 1934, Du Bois wrote an essay for *The Crisis* entitled "Segregation." In it, Du Bois again advocated that African Americans should join in economic and educational cooperation. If this cooperation meant segregation then, he said, they shouldn't be afraid of that term. White took immediate exception to Du Bois's statements. He was afraid that segregationists might use Du Bois's words to justify further segregation. He also said that the NAACP had always fought for total desegregation.

Du Bois disputed this view, pointing out that the association had supported separate training camps for African-American soldiers during the war. He also noted that the NAACP had long supported segregated schools and colleges.

Accusations flew back and forth between the two men. Despite their argument, Du Bois maintained that the principles both men supported were much the same. He believed they both wanted equal rights, and only differed in the methods they advocated for gaining those rights.

But the dispute had become too big and too personal to reconcile. Matters came to a head in May 1934 when the NAACP Board of Directors approved the following statement: *"The Crisis* is the organ of the Association and no salaried officer of the Association shall criticize the policy, work, or officers of the Association in the pages of *The Crisis."* The message was clear: Du Bois needed to fall in line.

John Hope, president of Atlanta University, had tried to persuade his old friend Du Bois to return to the university for years. After twenty-four years at the NAACP, Du Bois felt the time had clearly come for him to take his leave. As he later remembered, Pope promised him "leisure for thought and writing, and freedom of expression, so far, of course, as Georgia would permit it."

Du Bois resigned his position at the NAACP and returned to Atlanta as head of the department of sociology. From that position, he made ambitious plans for the future. He wrote, "These plans in my mind fell into three categories; first, with leisure to write, I wanted to fill in the background of certain historical studies concerning the Negro race; secondly, I wanted to establish at Atlanta University a scholarly journal of comment and research on world race problems; finally, I wanted to restore in some form at Atlanta, the systematic study of the Negro problem."

Du Bois was sixty-six when he returned to Atlanta, an age when many people begin to think about retirement. But Du Bois was far from ready to give up his work. Over the next ten years, he wrote and published books, articles, and essays. One of his major works from that time was *Black Reconstruction in America: 1860–1880*. It was a social history of African Americans in the turbulent time after the Civil War. In it, Du Bois drew upon his firsthand knowledge of that time from the summers he spent in Tennessee while a student at Fisk. Reconstruction was only ten years past when Du Bois taught at the little country school.

The problems that Reconstruction was meant to deal with began even before the war was over, as early as

1861. Advancing Union armies were confronted by hundreds of fugitive slaves who, often for lack of a better (or safer) option, fell in behind the troops as they marched. By the time Lincoln emancipated the slaves on January 1, 1863, the stream of fugitives had risen to a flood. Commanders on the battlefields inquired repeatedly as to how to feed and clothe what had become an army of refugees.

At first, able-bodied men were enlisted in the Union army or employed as laborers. The women and children were herded into camps. Eventually, more than fifty charitable organizations combined to provide relief for former slaves. By 1864, it was apparent that the federal government would have to act on a large scale. In February 1865, the Bureau of Refugees, Freedmen, and Abandoned Lands was created. This entity became known simply as the Freedmen's Bureau and was instrumental in the successes—and some of the failures—of Reconstruction.

The goal of Reconstruction had been to restore order to the former Confederate states, to provide them with stable Unionist governments, to help the people of those states begin to rebuild, and to help freed slaves integrate into society and adjust to their new status. Reconstruction was controversial from the outset. From its official beginning in 1865 to its end in 1877, Reconstruction tried to shift the balance of power in the South from wealthy white landowners to small farmers and workers, blacks and whites alike. For a brief period of time, the South elected an unprecedented number of African

Americans to positions in government, and great strides toward equality were made. But corruption in government on the state and federal level resulted in the passage of laws that eroded voting and other rights for African Americans. After Reconstruction ended, its gains were quickly lost and most African Americans were worse off than they had been at the end of the war.

By 1935, the prevailing view in America was that Reconstruction had failed because newly freed slaves were unprepared and unsuited to handle freedom and the responsibilities of government. Reconstruction was portrayed as a punishment inflicted on the vanquished South by vindictive and heartless Northerners who hoped only to profit from the war and who implemented corrupt and unfair governments.

Du Bois soundly rejected that school of thought and argued instead that in many ways Reconstruction had proved African Americans could take leadership roles in their communities. He admitted that the problems of Reconstruction were real and extensive but contended that the reasons given for the failures were misleading. He pointed to the violence carried out by racist organizations, including the Ku Klux Klan, as evidence that Reconstruction governments were harassed and attacked, not inherently incompetent.

Du Bois's book was a landmark piece of scholarship. It began a serious reconsideration of Reconstruction and it represents today the generally accepted view of that time in American history. Du Bois's faith in educa-

Du Bois *(far left)* at Atlanta University with *(from left to right)* actor Richard B. Harrison, Atlanta University president John Hope, and director of the Commission on Interracial Cooperation, Will W. Alexander.

tion was, in some small way, borne out by the success of his book.

Still, Du Bois faced a great many challenges in his quest to solve the problem of the color line. University president Hope died unexpectedly in 1936 and left Du Bois without his main support in Atlanta. The two friends had begun an effort to restart the Atlanta Conferences, but money was scarce. America was still sunk in the Great Depression, despite the efforts of President Franklin Delano Roosevelt and his New Deal plan to create jobs.

The year that Hope died, Du Bois took advantage of an offer from the Oberlaender Trust to embark on a world tour. The trust was actually funding a journey to Germany and Austria to study the schools there, but Du Bois packed his bags and spent seven months abroad visiting the Soviet Union, China, and Japan as well.

As before, Du Bois's trip overseas was instructive. He was delighted by the progress he saw in the Soviet Union. His belief in the equalizing power of communism was reinforced by his visit and the way things looked while he was there. But the darker side of the Soviet Union's experiment was already starting to show, and soon the world would be forced to confront the fact that communism under Joseph Stalin meant government by an oppressive and violent dictatorship.

By the mid-1930s, world events made it clear that further conflict was on the horizon. The peace treaties that ended World War I had only served to create more tension between the various countries involved. The Great Depression that so powerfully affected the United States was also felt abroad, destabilizing economies and governments in Europe. The rise to power of Adolf Hitler and his Nazi party in Germany, as well as the aggressive land grabbing of the fascist Benito Mussolini in Italy, all spelled trouble ahead.

Du Bois spent much of his time abroad in Germany. Du Bois was present for the 1936 Olympic Games, which were marred by Hitler's attempt to use them to prove his theories of racial superiority. Ironically, it was Jesse Owens, a black American, who was the star of the games, winning four gold medals. Still, Hitler and his party continued their efforts to brand ethnic groups, especially Jewish people, as inferior. Like many observers, Du Bois was appalled by the Nazi's growing anti-Semitic

Jesse Owens at start of his record-breaking 200-meter race at the 1936 Olympics in Berlin. *(Library of Congress)*

campaign. When he returned to the States, Du Bois said firmly, "There has been no tragedy in modern times equal in its awful effects to the fight on the Jew in Germany. It is an attack on civilization, comparable only to such horrors as the Spanish Inquisition and the African Slave Trade."

Though Du Bois was outraged by the dangerous and racist policies of Nazi Germany, he came home more determined than ever that the United States should avoid involvement in any possible conflict in Europe. This was a widely shared sentiment in the 1930s. America was still reeling from the previous war and from the effects of the Depression. Du Bois further took the position that the suffering Hitler inflicted was hardly different from the suffering caused by colonialism around the globe. When he said that the "British Empire has caused more human misery than Hitler will cause if he lives a hundred years," he meant to point out that Hitler's programs were not unique. The colonization of Africa had resulted in the deaths of millions of Africans and the indescribable abuse of millions more. Du Bois had great sympathy for the people of Germany, but he would not forget that his people had suffered too, and no one lifted a hand to help them.

Returning home to Atlanta, Du Bois continued to immerse himself in his work. He published a tremendous amount of books and articles, including *Black Folk Then and Now* and *Dusk of Dawn: An Essay toward an Autobiography of a Race Concept.* He also began a new publication called *Phylon,* a quarterly journal devoted to race issues. Despite these achievements, he still could not find the money to restart the Atlanta conferences.

*Black Folk Then and Now* is a cultural and economic history of African Americans. It begins with the roots of the slave trade and traces the experiences of African Americans through the first third of the twentieth century. The book is determinedly pro-Marx and works to show how the struggles of blacks in America parallel the struggles of an oppressed people in a capitalist system. Du Bois was always interested in the role the economy played in the fight for freedom.

*Dusk of Dawn* was written when Du Bois was seventy years old and serves in many ways as an autobiography. In it, he tells the story of his life and the development of his view that the central problem of the modern world is the color line. He also reconsiders some of his earlier solutions to that problem, including the concept of the talented tenth. Based on his experiences, Du Bois concluded he had been wrong about the talented tenth. Though he still hoped those African Americans who had secure employment and good education would be able to assume leadership positions, he was more critical of their ability to help others. Du Bois believed that a capitalist economy, with its focus on competition, would always encourage successful people to look up instead of down.

# Eight

# War and Peace

World War II began in the fall of 1939 when Germany invaded Poland. Americans watched anxiously from the other side of the ocean, hoping to avoid becoming embroiled in another global conflict. Du Bois, like many Americans, did not want to see American troops sent to Europe again.

Over the next months, German troops occupied Denmark, Norway, the Netherlands, Belgium, and France. Other Eastern European countries, including Hungary, Romania, Bulgaria, Yugoslavia, and Greece, either joined with Germany voluntarily or were beaten into submission. Soon, Great Britain stood alone in the fight against Hitler.

In June of 1941, German troops moved into the Soviet Union. Most observers hoped the Russian military would take some of the pressure off England's beleaguered forces, but it was already becoming clear the British would need American help or all of Europe would fall.

Du Bois's antiwar views changed after the invasion of Russia—but not for the usual reasons. He urged his fellow Americans to support sending troops to Russia's aid. Du Bois published an editorial explaining, "The war between Russia and Germany [reorients] all our thinking. The hopes of the modern world rest on the survival of the new conception of politics and industry which Russia represents."

Six months later, the Japanese launched a surprise attack against the American naval fleet at Pearl Harbor, and the United States was once again at war.

Du Bois saw the war as a great chance for the world. He had high hopes that by ending the tyrannous rules of Hitler, Mussolini, Francisco Franco in Spain, and the imperialist government in Japan, the resulting peace would further the spread of democracy and lend more credence to the struggle for Africa to rid itself of colonial rule. Democracy, to Du Bois, meant more than just universal suffrage and the end of Jim Crow laws. He believed a truly democratic society would end injustice and bring an end to unemployment and poverty.

Du Bois's political beliefs sometimes seem a little confusing. He was against war yet supported his country in the fight against fascism, which he saw as a greater evil. He believed in democracy as it represented a free society yet embraced communism as a more equitable way of distributing society's wealth. Du Bois admitted that his ideas and beliefs changed with circumstances through the years. Each new experience or development became a chance for him to find another, possibly better, way to achieve his firmly fixed ultimate goal: a just and equal society for everyone.

As World War II raged in Europe, Du Bois drew up a plan for restarting his Atlanta conferences and bringing more attention to the plight of African Americans. His designs were brought up short, however, when he was asked to retire from Atlanta University. Du Bois speaks of this blow in his autobiography: "Without a word of warning I found myself at the age of 76 without employment and with less than $5,000 of savings. . . . [my] life was thrown into confusion. I felt the world tottering beneath my feet and I fought back in despair."

Du Bois suspected that his sudden forced retirement was a carefully planned scheme to get a troublesome old man out of the picture. He believed Atlanta University was trying to eliminate him the way Walter White and the NAACP had. Once again, Du Bois's outspokenness and his disagreements with those in power cost him his livelihood. Atlanta University eventually voted to give Du Bois a small pension, but for the moment, his future looked bleak. Salvation came from an unexpected quarter: Du Bois's old sparring partner, Walter White.

By the spring of 1944, the tide of the war seemed to be turning in the favor of the Allied powers. The NAACP, like Du Bois, hoped that the end of the war would bring the chance to draw the world's attention to the plight of blacks around the world. White wrote to Du Bois to ask him to return to the NAACP as director of special research. His job would be to prepare material for the anticipated peace conference so that people of African descent would be represented there too.

Du Bois had to be encouraged to accept the position he was offered. He had left the NAACP on bad terms in 1934, and now, ten years later, he was uncertain about renewing his working relationship with Walter White.

A series of letters went back and forth between Du Bois and the NAACP board to negotiate his return. Du Bois later remembered, "I asked a salary of $5,000; two offices, one for myself and library and one for my secretary; I wanted leisure to write and assured them that I expected no role in the executive department of the organization; that I would be glad to revive the Pan-African movement

W. E. B. Du Bois in his late seventies. *(Library of Congress)*

and give general attention to the foreign aspects of the race problem." When his requests were agreed to, Du Bois packed his bags and moved back to New York in September of 1944.

Du Bois arrived at the NAACP offices to find that he, his secretary, and his 2,500 books were to be crowded into a tiny room near Walter White's offices. No amount of polite complaint secured the promised offices. In addition, it soon became apparent that White anticipated the seventy-six-year-old Du Bois would be ready for semi-retirement. Du Bois, on the other hand, said he felt no lessening of his ability to do serious and important work. It appeared to Du Bois that White only wanted him as window dressing, a famous name to write a few speeches now and then. But Du Bois planned to jump into new efforts on behalf of Pan-Africanism as well as to write and publish.

World War II officially ended in the fall of 1945. A new organization, the United Nations (UN), was created to oversee the peace process. Du Bois took an active part in it, attending meetings and writing dozens of newspaper articles about it. He thought the UN might help encourage national independence in Asia, Africa, and the Caribbean, but was also afraid the United States might join with other capitalist nations against the Soviet Union.

Du Bois's renewed work for Pan-Africanism had more satisfying results. Long-time Pan-Africanism leader George Padmore called a Fifth Pan-African Congress

for October 1945. After some initial disagreement about
the timing of it, Du Bois threw his support and considerable energies into the planning and execution of the
congress in Manchester, England.

Two hundred delegates met to plan the future of
postwar nationalist movements. They were leading trade
unionists, politicians, and radical intellectuals from all
over the world. The delegates drafted resolutions calling
for the right to organize free labor unions as well as the
right for home rule in Africa. They discussed ways to
alleviate the poverty and illiteracy of the African people.
Du Bois was welcomed and praised as the father of Pan-
Africanism and his voice was heard strongly in all the
discussions and decisions. He gave a stirring speech in
which he outlined the congress's goal: "It is perfectly
clear . . . what the African peoples want. They want the
right to govern themselves. . . . We must impress upon
the world that it must be Self Government."

When Du Bois returned to New York, he found himself in continued conflict with Walter White. The NAACP
was essentially divided into two parts: the executive
side, run by White, which dealt with membership, publications, local organizations, and other non-legal issues; and the legal department, which had separate
funding and separate offices. The NAACP's legal department had achieved outstanding success in using the
courts to challenge segregation. These challenges also
gave rise to more conflict between Du Bois and Walter
White.

Du Bois's worldwide fame meant he was often asked to contribute his opinion, his testimony, or his writing to various causes. When his views diverged from the official position of the NAACP, Du Bois did not censor himself. White was angry because he believed Du Bois had a responsibility as a representative of the NAACP to promote the association's views. Du Bois demurred, arguing he had a right, as a private citizen, to his own views. Du Bois responded to White's criticism by complaining that the NAACP's secretary was exerting too much influence over the organization. The two continued to snipe at each other. Du Bois's popularity and high profile was one of the main reasons White could not remove him from the organization.

In spite of his advancing age, Du Bois maintained an active schedule during these years. He later wrote a summary of his activities between 1944 and 1948: "I attended the Fifth Pan-African Congress in England, wrote two books on colonies and Africa, edited two others and wrote many articles, pamphlets and newspaper columns. I attended several conferences and traveled 20,000 miles to deliver 150 lectures on subjects connected with my work for the NAACP as I conceived it." Du Bois also served as an instructor for two semesters at the New School for Social Research in New York and was a guest speaker at Vassar, Yale, and Princeton universities.

In the years after World War II, one of Du Bois's concerns was the development of the United States' relationship with the Soviet Union. The two countries had an uneasy alliance during the war, but in its aftermath became enmeshed in a conflict over the spread of communism. Du Bois, in keeping with his political and economic philosophy, spoke out strongly in favor of the Communist system. He published a flood of essays and newspaper articles explaining his opposition to colonialism, his support for socialism, and his admiration of the Soviet Union. As the tension between the United States and the Soviet Union grew, so did the tension between Du Bois, White, and the NAACP board.

Du Bois's fame made him all the more dangerous to Walter White. If Du Bois's radical leftist political views came to be associated with the NAACP, the organization might be labeled Communist. While the NAACP might agree with Du Bois on many issues, they did not want to be identified with Soviet communism. When Du Bois announced his intention to support the Progressive Party's candidate for president, Henry Wallace, in the 1948 election, it was clear a break was near. White and the NAACP supported the incumbent Harry Truman. White issued a statement promising to enforce a previously ignored rule that no salaried employee of the association should take part in politics.

Du Bois did not take this announcement lightly. He later wrote, "I replied that I certainly would be careful not to appear to speak for the NAACP nor to take the time for active political work; but I assumed that I had the right to vote and tell my choice; that this was what the NAACP had stood for during 30 years."

Henry Wallace, pictured here on the cover of *Time* during his 1948 bid for the presidency as the Progressive Party candidate, was a longtime supporter of organized labor. During the campaign, Harry Truman was able to exploit the growing anti-Communist sentiment in America in order to defeat his more Socialist-leaning opponent.

Soon after this, Du Bois spoke at a nonpolitical meeting in Philadelphia, at which he asked the audience to vote for Wallace. He said later that he was careful to explain that his remarks did not reflect any official stand of the NAACP, but White still took exception. Then, a memo written by Du Bois that was critical of Walter White was printed in *The New York Times*. Someone other than Du Bois had leaked the material, but the damage was done. Du Bois was asked to leave his position at the NAACP, again.

This time many of Du Bois's friends and supporters protested his removal. Some of them wanted him to lead a campaign to reorganize the NAACP. But he was unwilling to undertake what he called "the duty of younger persons." Instead, he turned his attention to finding work.

Du Bois's wife, Nina, had lived with their daughter Yolande in Baltimore for several years. In 1946, she had suffered a paralytic stroke and required expensive nursing care. Du Bois's retirement income from Atlanta University and the royalties from his books were not sufficient to allow him to provide for his wife and carry on his work. Without a steady source of income, Du Bois faced financial disaster. A $5,000 donation from a philanthropist helped bridge the gap, but Du Bois knew he needed further means of support.

Relief came in the form of a position as honorary vice chairman of the Council on African Affairs. The council would not pay Du Bois a salary, but he would be provided an office and a secretary. The council was devoted to serving Africa in every way possible. Du Bois jumped at the chance to continue his Pan-African work and to continue to reach out to the people.

In 1948, when Du Bois arrived on the scene, the Council on African Affairs had just come out of its own political upheaval when it had been put on the U.S. Attorney General's list of subversive organizations. President Truman's fight against the spread of communism was undertaken at home as well as abroad. In an effort to seek out subversive elements in the United States, Truman had given FBI director J. Edgar Hoover broad powers to search for Communist spies and sympathizers.

While the Council on African Affairs was not a Communist organization, some of its members were Communists. Paul Robeson, a former singer and actor and one of the founders of the Council, felt that the political or religious beliefs of the Council's members were their own business, as long as the Council's actions were legal. He did not discourage his employees from choosing membership in the Communist Party or from expressing pro-Soviet views. Du Bois appreciated Robeson's open-mindedness and dived happily into his new job.

Once again turning to the power of the written word, Du Bois wrote dozens of articles and essays supporting the council's activities and advocating peace with the Soviet Union. Now that he no longer represented the NAACP, he was free to express his views. He was also able to participate in national and international peace movements. In a March 1949 speech at the Cultural and Scientific Conference for World Peace in New York City, Du Bois defended his new position: "We know and the saner nations know that we are not traitors nor conspirators; and far from plotting force and violence it is precisely force and violence that we bitterly oppose. This conference was not called to defend communism or socialism nor the American way of life. It was called to promote peace!"

A month later, Du Bois was invited to attend the Paris World Congress for Peace. The Congress attracted 2,000 delegates, all of whom welcomed Du Bois enthusiastically. He was astonished and delighted to be applauded and thanked for his years of work in favor of peace and justice. But that warm reception soon turned cold after Paul Robeson took the podium.

Robeson's controversial speech drew parallels between the colonial policy of the U.S.

The great actor and activist, Paul Robeson.

government and those of Hitler. He declared that African Americans should not fight against the Soviet Union because they would be acting against their own interests if they did so. Though Robeson denied being a member of the Communist Party, he had long been sympathetic to the Soviet Union, which he saw as supportive of African Americans and equality. Du Bois backed up Robeson's speech, and the two men returned to the United States to be vilified as Communists by blacks and whites alike. Du Bois was roundly criticized for his support of Robeson.

Still, Du Bois had the courage of his convictions. Despite the strong opposition to his Communist sympa-

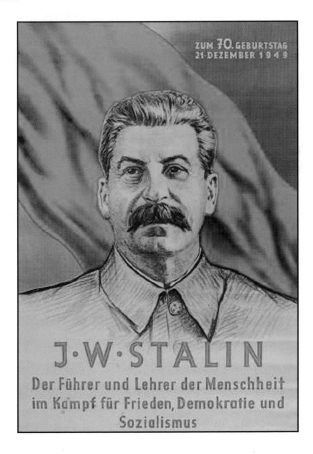

thies, Du Bois did not back down. That summer, he was the only American to accept an invitation to a Peace Congress held in the Soviet Union. He began his speech there by saying, "I represent millions of citizens of the United States who are just as opposed to war as you are. But it is not easy for American citizens either to know the truth about the world or to express it."

Stalin used propaganda throughout Eastern Europe and Asia to promote himself and the USSR. This poster, commemorating Stalin's seventieth birthday, reads: "The leader and teacher of humanity in the fight for peace, democracy and socialism."

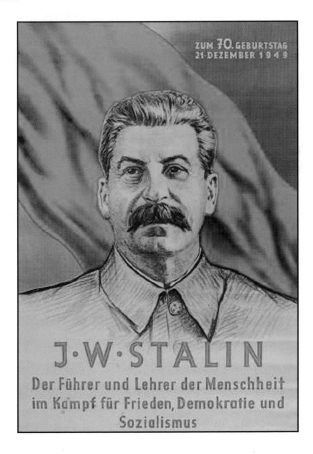

While it might have been true that the people Du Bois spoke to were in favor of peace, the Russian government, led by the autocratic ruler Joseph Stalin, was making peace difficult. The USSR was expanding its influence over Eastern Europe and still claimed control over the northern part of the Korean peninsula. Stalin's version of communism resulted in purges, particularly of Jewish intellectuals. Yet at the time, not everyone realized the danger the Soviet Union posed, nor did they fully understand the violence Stalin had perpetrated against his own people. As this information began to seep out, those who had embraced communism were shaken. But Du Bois held firm in his beliefs—beliefs that would cost him greatly in the years to come.

# Nine

# The Peace Information Center

In the spring of 1950, eighty-two-year-old W. E. B. Du Bois joined with other activists to found the Peace Information Center (PIC). Its purpose was to keep Americans informed of the work being done in the U.S. and abroad to promote peace. Du Bois was appointed chairman of the Advisory Council. The PIC was a small organization but soon made a huge impact.

One of its first acts was to print and circulate petitions supporting an appeal that had originated at a meeting of the World Partisans of Peace in Stockholm in March 1950, which called for banning the nuclear bomb. The drive continued for over two years, and half a billion people worldwide signed the petition.

That summer brought more challenges into Du Bois's life. Nina, his wife of more than fifty years, died on July 1, after five years of illness. Though the couple had long lived separately, Du Bois missed his wife's support and companionship. He was lonely, in part because he had outlived many of his good friends. But he did have one friend who looked after him and sought his advice. Her name was Shirley Graham.

Shirley Graham had first met Du Bois in 1920 when she was just thirteen years old. Her father, a minister, had invited the famous man to speak at his church. Du Bois stayed at the parsonage with the Graham family. Shirley was the oldest of five children and the only girl. She was quite impressed by the kindly man who answered all her questions and told stories to her little brothers.

Years passed before the two met again. Graham married, had two sons, and was widowed. She managed to attend and graduate from Oberlin College. Eventually, her work for civil rights brought her and Du Bois back in touch, and he became her mentor. They became close friends and corresponded for many years.

By the time of Nina's death, Graham and Du Bois had been working together or in the same circles for several years. She knew the pain Du Bois was feeling, having lost both her husband and her older son. Her kindness and concern for Du Bois's physical well-being were a great help to him that fall as he faced two challenges.

In August of 1950, the PIC received a letter from the Justice Department instructing it to register as an agent of a foreign interest as directed by the terms of the Foreign Agents Registration Act of 1938. This act was designed to monitor the influence of other countries on organizations operating within the United States. How the determination was made that the PIC was an agent of a foreign interest is not clear, but the Justice Department insisted that the registration statement be done quickly as the PIC had been operating without being registered for some time. Although not specifically mentioned, it was clear they considered the PIC to be an agent of the Soviet Union.

Du Bois received this news by cable as he traveled home from yet another peace conference in Eastern Europe. He received another cable at the same time. This one was from the American Labor Party, asking Du Bois to run for a seat in the United States Senate.

The American Labor Party had been formed in 1936 in order to support President Roosevelt's New Deal and any candidates who backed it. The ALP had split in 1944 over the issue of communism, with those remaining members strongly in favor of the Russian government. The party had lost members after the 1948 election, but retained enough power to influence races in New York.

Although Du Bois had little political experience and brought a distinctly radical reputation with him—not good qualifications for a candidate—he was eventually convinced that running for public office would give him a way to promote his ideas about peace. He also hoped that his candidacy might help the reelection campaign of Vito Marcantonio, an American Labor Party congressman from New York. Du Bois admired Marcantonio

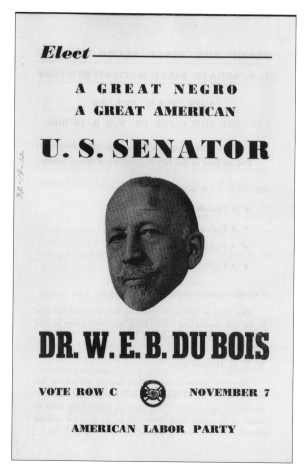

An election poster from Du Bois's campaign for the Senate in 1950. *(Special Collections and Archives, W.E.B. Du Bois Library, University of Massachusetts Amherst)*

for his tough stand against the Cold War in the House of Representatives.

The Cold War was the term for the tension between the United States and the Soviet Union that began with the end of World War II. At that time, the Korean peninsula had been divided in half—North Korea had been given to the Communist Soviet Union to control, and the

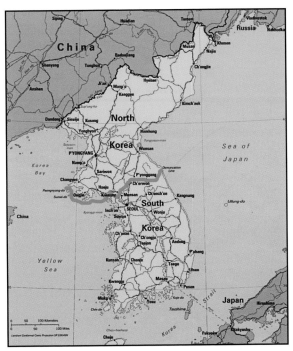

This map shows the Korean peninsula in 1950. The red line marks the delineation between North and South Korea, running roughly along the 38th parallel.

United States backed the new South Korean government. In June of 1950, North Korean troops surged over the border into South Korea. Fear of a Communist takeover led the United States to commit troops on behalf of South Korea. In the meantime, concerns about Communist expansion were more widespread than ever.

Du Bois, like Marcantonio, had few concerns about the spread of communism. As a result, he had no illusions about his chances of actually winning the election: "I went into the campaign for Senator knowing well from the first that I did not have a ghost of a chance for election, and that my efforts would bring me ridicule at best and jail at worst. On the other hand, I did have a message which was worth attention, and which in the long run could not fail to have influence."

Du Bois gave ten speeches and seven radio broadcasts during the campaign. Although not a long campaign by today's standards, it was long enough for Du Bois to have his say about the Cold War. He summed up his message by saying, "The most sinister evil of this day is the widespread conviction that war is inevitable and that there is no time left for discussion." He went on to insist that "two things have become increasingly clear; one, that the costs of war have become too great for any nation to pay, no matter what the alternative; and two, that in war as now carried on, there can be no victorious party."

Du Bois and Marcantonio both lost in November, but Du Bois attracted a surprisingly large number of votes, given his positions. Five million votes were cast in New York, and Du Bois was the choice of over 205,000 people. He said later that since he hadn't expected to win, "I would not have been surprised if no more than 10,000 persons had voted for me. I was astonished by a vote of 205,729, a vote from men and women of courage, without the prejudice against color which I always expect and usually experience." He pronounced himself happy that so many had joined him in demanding peace and civil rights for all.

During the election season, the PIC had responded to the Justice Department's request by letter and in person, doing everything it could to show that the PIC had never been nor intended to become an agent for the Soviet Union or any other foreign power. Still, the government continued to insist that the group register. Finally, financial and governmental pressures became too much. On October 12, 1950, the PIC board voted to dissolve the organization. It took several months to finish up the center's business affairs. The government interpreted the continuing activity as proof that the PIC was just avoiding registration.

A federal grand jury met in Washington, D.C., to investigate the PIC and determine if any of its officers should be indicted for failure to comply with the law. On February 9, 1951, the jury handed down five indictments against officials of the PIC. Du Bois was one of the people named. He and the others faced a possible fine of $10,000 each and up to five years in federal prison.

Five days after the news of the indictment broke, Du Bois and Shirley Graham were secretly married on Valentine's Day 1951. They had planned to marry anyway, and the possibility that Du Bois might go to jail provided a certain urgency. Two days later, the PIC officers were formally arraigned in Federal District Court in Washington, D.C. Du Bois and the others were fingerprinted, searched, and handcuffed. Du Bois's handcuffs were removed after his attorney protested. He posted $1,000 bail and was allowed to go home.

Du Bois's arrest caused shock and anger around the world. A lecture tour was arranged for the summer to

Du Bois and Shirley Graham's wedding on February 14, 1951. *(Special Collections and Archives, W.E.B. Du Bois Library, University of Massachusetts Amherst)*

raise money to pay for his defense. Vito Marcantonio, the former congressman and a lawyer, offered to donate his services to the PIC legal team.

The lecture tour took place in June and September of 1951. Du Bois and Shirley Graham traveled across the country to speak to peace groups, African-American organizations, churches, and unions. The program began with Mrs. Du Bois, who described the Peace Information Center, related the nature of the indictments, and explained the penalties the defendants might face if found guilty.

After some local speakers, Du Bois would give the main speech. His wife said later of his planned speeches, "That major address was to give me considerable concern. For as he lashed out at war's greedy profiteers, as he exposed the methods by which honest people were being frightened and oppressed, as he told of the organized violence of imperialism at home and abroad, I trembled lest he be carried off to jail even before the trial."

Du Bois remained free, and the lecture tours raised more than $35,000 for the defense fund. The trial was delayed several times. Du Bois was offered the chance to take a plea bargain, but he refused, maintaining his innocence.

In his autobiography, Du Bois recorded his feelings about the first day of his trial: "I have faced during my life many unpleasant experiences . . . But nothing has so cowed me as that day, November 8, 1951, when I took my seat in a Washington courtroom as an indicted criminal. I was not a criminal. I had broken no law, consciously or unwittingly."

Judge James McGuire was assigned to the trial, and he quickly poked holes in the prosecution's case. He was politically conservative and a by-the-book kind of judge. McGuire reminded the lawyers from the outset that the case did not rest on the political opinions of the accused. The prosecution had to prove that the PIC had some connection to a foreign country and was representing that country in the U.S. Only by proving that connection could it be shown that the PIC had violated the law by not registering under the Foreign Agents Registration Act.

The prosecution had claimed to have such proof for months; Du Bois and the others waited to hear the evidence. Du Bois later said that although he knew there could be no proof that the accusation was true, he wondered if someone had lied or if there was other made-up evidence. His fears were put to rest on the

W. E. B. and Shirley Du Bois, center, stand with other Peace Information Center defendants Kyrle Elkin, Sylvia Soloff, and Abbott Simon in front of the federal courthouse in Washington, D.C., before their arraignment. *(Special Collections and Archives, W.E.B. Du Bois Library, University of Massachusetts Amherst)*

afternoon of November 20, when Judge McGuire, to the astonishment of the courtroom observers, announced that he was granting an acquittal. He said that the prosecution had provided no convincing reason to think that the PIC had any connection with a foreign country, and therefore there had been no reason for the group to register, making the charge of failure to register unfounded.

The quick end to the trial stunned everyone in the courtroom. At first, Du Bois thought that he had misunderstood the judge's words. Shirley Du Bois said that her first response was laughter, perhaps hysterical in nature. But the ruling was real, and soon Du Bois and his wife were on their way home, free after nine months of intense preparation for the trial. Yet despite being acquitted of the charges against him, Du Bois would find his reputation had suffered lasting damage. The next few years would be difficult ones for the old radical.

Before his trial, the NAACP had reduced Du Bois's annual pension from $2,400 to $1,200 without any notice. This blow, combined with the money he spent on his defense, put a severe strain on Du Bois's bank account. Though he continued to write and kept a sheaf of speeches at hand, he was no longer invited to talk, and the periodicals that had previously asked for his articles and essays were suddenly silent.

Du Bois may have been acquitted, but he was far from forgiven. His show of support for the Soviet Union kept him under watch by government officials. A few months after the trial was over, he applied for a visa to attend a peace conference in Brazil. His request was denied, and the State Department confiscated his passport and that of his wife. A few months after that, Du Bois and Shirley traveled to Toronto to speak at the Canadian Peace Congress. As soon as they arrived, they were detained by the authorities, then forcibly sent back to the United States.

As always, Du Bois turned to the written word to help him through this difficult time. He never gave up believing that by sharing his story, he could teach people. *In Battle for Peace: the Story of My 83rd Birthday* was published in 1952. It described his arrest and his trial, and explained his perspectives on communism, socialism, and democracy. Du Bois wanted to make it clear that he believed in democracy, but that he could not ignore the promise of equality he believed that communism offered. The book had the unintended effect of increasing the government's attention on Du Bois, because in it he thanked members of the Communist Party for their support.

To be an admitted Communist in the 1950s in America was to be vilified as dangerous and subversive. Soon after Du Bois published *In Battle for Peace,* Joseph McCarthy began his famous hearings in the Senate. People suspected of being Communists or Communist sympathizers were asked to come forward to testify. Those who refused—for whatever reason—could be jailed. Careers were ruined and a climate of fear ruled America.

Du Bois was unafraid to speak out against oppression. *In Battle for Peace* documented his own experiences with government investigation: "The secret police swarmed in my neighborhood asking about my visitors; whether I entertained and whom. . . . My manuscripts and those of Shirley Graham were refused publication by reputable commercial publishers. My mail was tampered with or withheld."

The thing that troubled Du Bois the most, though, was the reaction of the members of the group that he had long thought of as the talented tenth. This group of successful African-American businessmen and professionals had not been supportive during Du Bois's indictment and trial, and generally distanced themselves from him even after the acquittal. Du Bois had hoped that his talented tenth would stand up as leaders in a free society, but now he felt abandoned by his own people. He said, "The colored children ceased to hear my name."

Even the NAACP seemed to have deserted Du Bois. The national office refused to let local branches invite Du Bois to speak. Du Bois later summed up his reaction to this rejection: "It was a bitter experience and I bowed before the storm. But I did not break. I continued to speak and write when and where I could. I faced my lowered income and lived within it. I found new friends and lived in a wider world than ever before—a world with no color line."

In a time when many prominent activists—black and white alike—gave in to the political climate to keep their jobs and lives intact, Du Bois refused to do so. He insisted that a country was not weakened by political dissent but was strengthened. He still believed that the rights of the worker were as important as the rights of the people and that a socialist society would almost automatically lead to freedom for African Americans. Du Bois's oft-expressed support for a third political party, as well as his outspoken support of the Soviet Union, meant he was sometimes viewed with suspicion. But Du Bois continued to speak and write against the repression of civil rights whenever and wherever he could. He had long ago stopped worrying about what other people thought of his beliefs.

# Ten

# Back to Africa

In the 1950s, as Du Bois battled discrimination for his Communist sympathies, the civil rights movement in America was gaining strength. The gains it made often came at great cost, however. This phase of the movement had been partially precipitated by the treatment soldiers received when they returned from World War II. Having fought for their country and watched their comrades give their lives in the name of freedom, African-American soldiers came back ready to be granted the equality they were promised under the Constitution. They wanted to be able to benefit from the booming economy, to attend college on the GI Bill, and to buy houses in the new neighborhoods springing up across the country. When they were met with continued discrimination, they became angry.

Legal challenges combined with social protest to seriously shake the status quo in America. Suddenly, the idea of equality was no longer a dream but a demand. Du Bois was an active participant in the fight for freedom. He taught a weekly class on African politics and history at Jefferson School of Social Science in New York City. He continued to work for the Council on African Affairs and wrote frequently about African affairs for publications around the country.

In 1954, the U.S. Supreme Court issued its landmark ruling in the case *Brown v. Board of Education.* The case began in Topeka, Kansas, in 1951 when a suit was filed against the board of education on behalf of a third-grader named Linda Brown because Linda had to walk a mile to her segregated black school even though there was a white school seven blocks from her house.

Justice Thurgood Marshall during his tenure on the U.S. Supreme Court.

The suit had the backing of the NAACP and chief counsel Thurgood Marshall, who would later be the first African American appointed to the Supreme Court. Marshall was instrumental in convincing the court to overturn its previous decision that allowed for separate but equal facilities by showing the court that segregation was inherently unequal. While it would take many years to desegregate America, *Brown* marked the beginning of the end of legal segregation. Du Bois said of the decision, "I have seen the impossible happen. It did happen on May 17, 1954."

Still, discrimination was rampant in America and particularly dangerous in the South. In 1955, fourteen-year-old Chicagoan Emmett Till was murdered because he allegedly whistled at a white woman in Mississippi. Till's mother brought her son's death to the attention of the nation by insisting that his mangled and brutalized body be shown in an open coffin to bear witness to the atrocity of his murder. Du Bois was among those who stood up to call for justice. He joined with other activist leaders to form the Provisional Committee for Justice in Mississippi. This organization pushed hard to convert the anger over Till's murder into a demand for voting rights for African Americans. Till's murderers were exonerated of the crime in part because they were tried by an all-white jury; blacks were barred from serving. Once they were acquitted, Till's killers offered a full confession in the pages of *Look* magazine, further flaming controversy and anger.

That same year in Montgomery, Alabama, the famous bus boycott began. Rosa Parks was arrested when she refused to give her bus seat to a white man, which was

This famous photograph shows Rosa Parks during her sit-in protest on a bus in Montgomery, Alabama. *(Library of Congress)*

in defiance of local segregation laws. Within days the local NAACP, backed by leaders including Martin Luther King Jr., began a boycott of the city's buses. It went on for nearly a year before the Supreme Court declared Alabama's state and local bus segregation laws unconstitutional.

During these years of burgeoning civil rights protest, Du Bois spoke out often and frankly. He was supported enthusiastically by his wife, who shared his ideals. He was sought out frequently by young black scholars who visited him to ask for advice. But true to form, Du Bois still stayed outside of the mainstream civil rights movement. In a time when African Americans across the country were joining together to protest racism and discrimination, Du Bois continued to be critical of the black middle class.

In 1957, Du Bois published the first of what would eventually be known as the *Black Flame* trilogy. All three novels dealt with the story of one black man, Mansart, who was the president of a small black college in Georgia. The books follow the fortunes of Mansart and his four children. Some critics saw them as too harsh and pessimistic in their views of the African-American middle class and its leaders. Du Bois had become increasingly disillusioned with black professionals and businessmen and women. The members of his much-talked about talented tenth had greatly disappointed him when it became clear that they were not taking up their roles as leaders—or at least not in the way he had imagined. The *Black Flame* trilogy was as politically motivated as Du Bois's other novels and reflected his continued desire to see African Americans triumph—his way.

As the civil rights movement continued to grow, Du Bois began to turn his attention away from America. Viewed either as an eccentric elder statesman or an outdated relic, Du Bois was valued by the movement mostly as an icon. Though he was still asked to write and to speak on issues, his perspectives and positions began to seem more and more out of step with mainstream views.

Du Bois's stance on communism was one of the main things that separated him from the crowd. While many

Americans had flirted with communism in the 1920s and '30s, to continue to voice support for the Soviet Union in the 1950s was different. In 1939, Soviet leader Joseph Stalin had signed a nonaggression pact with Adolf Hitler. Even after Hitler broke the agreement by invading Russia in 1941, most Communist sympathizers were disillusioned by Stalin's appeasement of the Nazi leader. When the world began to learn about the bloody purges Stalin had conducted to consolidate his power and the millions of Russians either killed or exiled to labor camps, even the most committed Communists reconsidered their positions. But not Du Bois. He had too much faith in communism's ability to erase color lines.

In 1958, the Supreme Court ruled that the State Department had no legal right to require anyone to sign a statement against communism before issuing them a passport. Passports were returned to Du Bois and his wife, and the couple made plans to travel abroad after eight years of restriction.

Their trip would last for almost a year and extended from Europe to China and the Soviet Union. Du Bois was received cordially throughout the world and was honored on several occasions for his work for Africa and for peace. Du Bois spent five months traveling throughout the Soviet Union and ten weeks in China. While in the Soviet Union, he talked with Soviet leader Nikita Khrushchev and received the Lenin Peace Prize.

Du Bois found the Soviet Union to have advanced greatly in education, science, and economics. "The Soviet

Union seems to me the only European country where people are not taught and encouraged to despise and look down on some class, group, or race," he said.

He was equally pleased at what he saw in China. Du Bois and his wife traveled throughout the People's Republic of China, visiting all the major cities. He talked with Chinese leader Mao Tse-tung for several hours and gave a lecture at Peking University on his ninety-first birthday. Du Bois was all praise for Chinese Communism. The progress and prosperity that he saw reinforced his idea that socialism was the only workable economic system.

Scholars later noted that Du Bois failed to see the contradictory signals that were already present in China. Less than ten years later, Mao would commence the Cultural Revolution to cleanse the Chinese Communist Party of his opponents. Thousands of intellectuals were imprisoned or murdered. The progress and prosperity Du Bois saw in China was a myth, but he was among those who were blinded by their beliefs.

While Du Bois was in the Soviet Union in December 1958, an All-African Conference was held in Accra, Ghana, in Africa. This was a continuation of the Pan-African Conferences, but the emphasis was to be on African participation. Du Bois had planned to go to Accra to address the conference but was ill. Shirley Du Bois went in his place and read his speech to the attendees while her husband stayed in a sanitarium near Moscow.

Du Bois's speech restated his conviction that capital-

Du Bois chats with Mao Tse-tung during Du Bois's visit to China. *(Special Collections and Archives, W.E.B. Du Bois Library, University of Massachusetts Amherst)*

ism could not endure. His wife delivered his description of socialism as the inevitable economic outcome: "But what is socialism? It is a disciplined economy and political organization in which the first duty of a citizen is to serve the state: and the state is not a selected aristocracy, or a group of self-seeking oligarchs who have seized wealth and power. No! The mass of workers with hand and brain are the ones whose collective destiny is the chief object of all effort."

Du Bois and his wife returned to the U.S. on July 1, 1959. Du Bois continued to write and speak. He worked hard on his autobiography, and continued to be critical of the black community. He thought that much of the black leadership or potential leadership had sold out to capitalism. He wanted black Americans to retain their African-American culture while leading their country in the fight for socialism.

In the summer of 1960, the Du Boises traveled to Ghana. Ghana was becoming a republic, and President Kwame Nkrumah invited the Du Boises to come to his inauguration. They spent six weeks there.

President Nkrumah and Du Bois had known each other for several years, but it was a surprise when Nkrumah asked his friend to undertake a huge scholarly project. The president wanted Du Bois to take charge of producing an *Encyclopaedia Africana,* and to make the project's headquarters in Accra, Ghana. This would be a multi-volume history of the African people. At first Du Bois said no—after all, he was ninety-two years old—

but it was the kind of project that Du Bois had longed to do his whole life. So the final answer was yes, and Du Bois began work in the fall of 1960. Just weeks later, news came that his daughter Yolande had suffered a heart attack and died. Du Bois was devastated by the loss of his only living child, and now had even less to hold him to America.

Du Bois had planned to remain in New York City while working on the *Encyclopaedia* and move to Accra sometime in 1962. This timetable changed abruptly in August 1961. For eight years the constitutionality of section eight of the Subversive Activities Control Act of 1950 had been challenged in the courts. Section eight required Communist Party members to register with the government and forbade them from applying for or using passports. In June 1961, the Supreme Court affirmed the constitutionality of section eight. It was announced that section eight would be enforced starting October 20, 1961.

Suddenly, it seemed possible that Du Bois might be placed under some form of house arrest because of his Communist beliefs. At the very least it was likely that his passport would be revoked.

Du Bois immediately contacted President Nkrumah, who urged the couple to come to Ghana without delay. At this time, Du Bois wasn't sure if this would be a permanent move, but their house was sold and all papers and manuscripts were packed.

There was one last bit of business to attend to before Du Bois left for his new life in Ghana. He officially joined the Communist Party. Although a great many people had considered him a Communist for years, he had never joined the organization.

Du Bois applied for admission in a letter to Gus Hall, the general secretary of the party: "I have been long and slow in coming to this conclusion, but at last my mind is settled," he said. Du Bois stated his beliefs clearly: "Today I have reached a firm conclusion: Capitalism cannot reform itself; it is doomed to self-destruction. No universal selfishness can bring social good to all. Communism—the effort to give all men what they need and to ask of each the best they can contribute—this is the only way of human life."

Less than a week after joining the Communist Party, Du Bois and his wife left for Africa. President Nkrumah had prepared a cottage for them outside Accra. The couple settled into a comfortable life. Du Bois worked on his autobiography and the *Encyclopaedia Africana*. He and Shirley entertained guests and participated in the local social life when his health permitted.

Old age and health problems at last began to restrict Du Bois's work schedule. For many years he had carefully adjusted his work and lived as healthfully as possible in order to maintain his ability to produce. In July 1962, he went to London for medical treatment and spent several months recuperating in Switzerland and China.

Du Bois returned to work in late 1962. Any plans he might have made to travel to the United States were thwarted when the U.S. consulate in Accra refused to

Du Bois enjoys a toast for his ninety-fifth birthday from Ghanaian president Kwame Nkrumah and his wife. *(Special Collections and Archives, W.E.B. Du Bois Library, University of Massachusetts Amherst)*

renew his passport because he was an official member of the Communist Party. He could be jailed in the United States for up to ten years for this crime.

Du Bois decided to finalize his connection with his adopted country. On February 17, 1963, W. E. B. Du Bois became a citizen of Ghana. He loved his new country and the people there loved him in return. But his health continued to fail, and in March 1963, he had to retire from his duties with the *Encyclopaedia*.

Du Bois died on August 27, 1963. He was ninety-five years old. Nkrumah held a state funeral for his friend and

This photograph of Du Bois was taken in Accra, Ghana, in 1963, not long before he died. *(Special Collections and Archives, W.E.B. Du Bois Library, University of Massachusetts Amherst)*

delivered a eulogy in a national radio broadcast. Nkrumah genuinely mourned the man he called "a great son of Africa." Tributes and condolences poured into Accra from all over the world. Only one consulate in Accra failed to pay its respects, and that was the American consulate. Du Bois's coffin was draped with the red, green, and gold flag of Ghana and carried three miles through the streets of Accra. Crowds of people followed to honor Du Bois.

News of Du Bois's death reached the United States on the morning of August 28. This was the same day as the historic March on Washington for Jobs and Freedom when over 250,000 people converged on Washington, D.C., to stand up for civil rights. When Du Bois's death was announced to the huge assembly, there was a moment of silence. Though he had not always followed the mainstream, Du Bois had always stood up for his beliefs and for his people.

Another famous black civil rights activist spoke of Du Bois's contributions in a speech given at a New York City Carnegie Hall tribute in 1968. Martin Luther King Jr. said of Du Bois, "His singular greatness lay in his quest for truth about his own people."

# Timeline

1868    Born February 23 in Great Barrington, Massachusetts.

1884    Graduates from Great Barrington High School.

1888    Graduates from Fisk University in Nashville, TN.

1890    Graduates with honors from Harvard University; begins graduate studies there.

1892    Studies at University of Berlin in Germany for two years.

1894    Teaches at Wilberforce University in Ohio until 1896; receives PhD degree from Harvard in 1896.

1896    Assistant instructor in sociology, University of Pennsylvania.

1897    Professor of economics and history, Atlanta University, until 1910.

1905    Founder and general secretary of the Niagara Movement through 1909.

1910    Director of publicity and research and member, board of directors, NAACP. Founder and publisher of *The Crisis* through 1934.

1919    Organizes first Pan-African Congress in Paris.

1926    First visit to the Soviet Union.

1933    Resigns from *The Crisis* and NAACP board.

1934    Chairman, Department of Sociology, Atlanta University, until 1934.

1936    Travels around the world.

1944    Returns to NAACP as director of special research.

1948    Forced out of NAACP; serves as co-chairman of Council on African Affairs.

1950   Chairman, Peace Information Center; runs for the U.S. Senate from New York as a member of the American Labor Party; indicted, tried, and acquitted as an officer of the Peace Information Center.

1958   Travels to the Soviet Union and China for a year.

1961   Joins the Communist Party of the United States; moves to Ghana, Africa.

1963   Becomes a citizen of Ghana; directs *Encyclopaedia Africana* project; dies in Accra, Ghana, on August 27.

# Sources

**CHAPTER ONE: A Challenging Start**

p.10, "I was fascinated . . ." W. E. B. Du Bois, *The Autobiography of W. E. B. Du Bois* (New York: International Publishers Co., Inc., 1968), 99.

p. 12-13, "He was small and beautiful . . ." Ibid., 71.

p. 17, "They sat down and talked . . ." Ibid., 98.

p. 19, "Now I was free . . ." Ibid., 102.

p. 20, "I was going into the South . . ." Ibid., 105.

**CHAPTER TWO: New Horizons**

p. 27, "Never before had I . . ." Ibid., 107.

p. 28, "The woman was furious . . ." Ibid., 121.

p. 29, "I had heard about . . ." Ibid., 114.

p. 31, "I ought to have . . ." Ibid., 134.

p. 32-33, "With them I led . . ." Ibid., 136.

p. 35, "I was, however . . ." Ibid.

p. 36, "My subject was . . ." Ibid., 146.

p. 36, "a naturally brave . . ." Ibid.

p. 36-37, "Du Bois handled his . . ." Ibid., 147.

p. 40, "They did not always . . ." Ibid., 157.

p. 41, "modified profoundly," Ibid., 156.

p. 41, "These are my plans . . ." Herbert Aptheker, ed., *W. E. B.*

*Du Bois: Against Racism* (Amherst: University of Massachusetts Press, 1985), 29.

## CHAPTER THREE: Finding His Place

p. 42, "I was not exacting . . ." Du Bois, *Autobiography,* 184.

p. 44, "No he won't . . ." Ibid., 186.

p. 44, "I went to Wilberforce . . ." Ibid.

p. 46, "We want to know . . ." Ibid., 197.

p. 46, "in the slums where . . ." Ibid., 195.

p. 46, "periodic spasms . . ." Ibid., 194.

p. 48, "First of all I . . ." Ibid., 198.

## CHAPTER FOUR: Atlanta

p. 52, "My real life work . . ." Ibid., 213.

p. 54, "It must be remembered . . ." Ibid., 219.

p. 55, "I tried to isolate . . ." Ibid., 208.

p. 56, "His death tore our . . ." Ibid., 281.

p. 62, "The problem of the . . . of modern civilization," David Levering Lewis, *W. E. B. Du Bois: Biography of a Race, 1868-1919* (New York: Henry Holt and Company, 1993), 251.

p. 62-63, "This was, of course . . ." Du Bois, *Autobiography,* 222.

p. 65, "In all things that . . ." Manning Marable, *W. E. B. Du Bois: Black Radical Democrat* (Boston: G.K. Hall & Co., 1986), 42.

p. 65, "The wisest among my . . ." Ibid.

p. 66, "this Tuskegee Machine was . . ." Du Bois, *Autobiography,* 239.

p. 66-67, "These methods have . . ." Ibid., 247.

p. 68, "These two theories of . . ." Ibid., 236.

p. 69, "I did not always . . ." Ibid., 248.

p. 70, "As between Trotter . . ." Herbert Aptheker, ed., *The*

*Correspondence of W. E. B. Du Bois*, vol. 1, *Selections, 1877-1934* (University of Massachusetts Press, 1973), 68.

## CHAPTER FIVE: The NAACP
p. 74, "1. Freedom of speech . . ." Du Bois, *Autobiography*, 249.
p. 76, "I bought a . . ." Ibid., 286.
p. 79, "This conference contained . . ." Ibid., 254.
p. 82, "The object of this . . ." Marable, *W. E. B. Du Bois*, 76.

## CHAPTER SIX: Gathering Storm
p. 93, "Let us, while this . . ." Ibid., 96.
p. 93, "I did not believe . . ." Du Bois, *Autobiography*, 274.
p. 97, "were chiefly memorable for . . ." Ibid., 291.
p. 101, "an extraordinary leader of . . ." Ibid., 273.

## CHAPTER SEVEN: Questions and Conflicts
p. 104, "Never before had . . ." Ibid., 290.
p. 104, "I believe in the . . ." Ibid.
p. 111, "He was absolutely . . ." Ibid., 293.
p. 112, "*The Crisis* is the . . ." Marable, *W. E. B. Du Bois*, 141.
p. 113, "leisure for thought . . ." Du Bois, *Autobiography*, 300.
p. 113, "These plans in my . . ." Ibid., 301.
p. 118, "There has been no . . ." Marable, *W. E. B. Du Bois*, 155.
p. 119, "British Empire has caused . . ." Ibid., 157.

## CHAPTER EIGHT: War and Peace
p. 122, "The war between Russia . . ." Ibid., 158.
p. 123, "Without a word of . . ." Du Bois, *Autobiography*, 323.
p. 124, "I asked a salary . . ." Ibid., 326.
p. 126, "It is perfectly clear . . ." Marable, *W. E. B. Du Bois*, 165.

p. 127, "I attended the Fifth . . ." Du Bois, *Autobiography*, 330.

p. 128, "I replied that I . . ." Ibid., 334.

p. 129-130, "the duty of younger . . ." Ibid., 335.

p. 131, "We know and the . . ." Ibid., 349-50.

p. 133, "I represent millions of . . ." Ibid., 351.


**CHAPTER NINE: The Peace Information Center**

p. 139-140, "I went into the . . ." Ibid., 361-62.

p. 140, "The most sinister evil . . ." Ibid., 362.

p. 140, "I would not have . . ." Ibid., 363.

p. 143, "That major address was . . ." Shirley Graham Du Bois, *His Day Is Marching On* (Philadelphia: J.B. Lippincott Company, 1971), 155.

p. 143, "I have faced during . . ." Du Bois, *Autobiography*, 379.

p. 147, "The secret police swarmed . . ." Ibid., 394.

p. 147, "The colored children . . ." Ibid., 395.

p. 147, "It was a bitter . . ." Ibid.


**CHAPTER TEN: Back to Africa**

p. 151, "I have seen the . . ." Gerald Horne, *Black & Red: W. E. B. Du Bois and the Afro-American Response to the Cold War, 1944-1963* (Albany, NY: State University of New York Press, 1986), 247.

p. 154-155, "The Soviet Union seems . . ." Marable, *W. E. B. Du Bois*, 205.

p. 157, "But what is socialism . . ." Shirley Graham Du Bois, *His Day Is Marching*, 372.

p. 159, "I have been long . . ." John Clarke, ed., *Black Titan: W. E. B. Du Bois* (Boston: Beacon Press, 1970), 304.

p. 161, "a great son of . . ." Marable, *W. E. B. Du Bois*, 213.

p. 162, "His singular greatness lay . . ." Clarke, *Black Titan*, 177.

# Bibliography

Aptheker, Herbert, ed. *W. E. B. Du Bois: Against Racism.* Amherst: University of Massachusetts Press, 1985.

———. *The Correspondence of W. E. B. Du Bois:* vol. 1, *Selections, 1877-1934.* Amherst: University of Massachusetts Press, 1973.

———. *Writings by W. E. B. Du Bois in Non-Periodical Literature.* Millwood, NY: Kraus-Thomson Organization Limited, 1982.

Broderick, Francis L. *W. E. B. Du Bois: Negro Leader in a Time of Crisis.* Stanford, CA: Stanford University Press, 1959.

Byerman, Keith. *Seizing the Word: History, Art, and Self in the Work of W. E. B. Du Bois.* Athens, GA: The University of Georgia Press, 1994.

Clarke, John Henrik, Esther Jackson, Ernest Kaiser, and J. H. O'Dell, eds. *Black Titan: W. E. B. Du Bois.* Boston: Beacon Press, 1970.

Dray, Philip. *At the Hands of Persons Unknown: The Lynching of Black America.* New York: Random House, 2002.

Du Bois, Shirley Graham. *His Day is Marching On: a Memoir of W. E. B. Du Bois.* Philadelphia: J.B. Lippincott Company, 1971.

Du Bois, W. E. B. *The Suppression of the African Slave-Trade to the United States of America, 1638-1870.* New York: Schocken Books, 1896.

———. *The Souls of Black Folk: Essays and Sketches.* Chicago: A.C. McClurg & Co., 1903.

———. *Darkwater: Voices From Within the Veil.* New York: AMS Press, Inc., 1920.

————. *Dusk of Dawn: An Essay Toward an Autobiography of a Race Concept.* New York: Schocken Books, 1968.

————. *The Autobiography of W. E. B. Du Bois.* New York: International Publishers Co., Inc., 1968.

————. *Black Reconstruction in America 1860-1880.* New York: Atheneum, 1979.

Ferguson, Blanche E. *Countee Cullen and the Negro Renaissance.* New York: Dodd, Mead & Company, 1966.

Foner, Philip, ed. *W. E. B. Du Bois Speaks: Speeches and Addresses 1890-1919.* New York: Pathfinder Press, 1970.

————. *W. E. B. Du Bois Speaks: Speeches and Addresses 1920-1963.* New York: Pathfinder Press, 1970.

Gaines, Kevin. *Uplifting the Race: Black Leadership, Politics, and Culture in the Twentieth Century.* Chapel Hill: The University of North Carolina Press, 1996.

Ginzburg, Ralph. *100 Years of Lynchings.* Baltimore: Black Classic Press, 1962.

Grant, Donald. *The Anti-Lynching Movement: 1883-1932.* San Francisco: R and E Research Associates, 1975.

Green, Dan and Edwin Driver, eds. *W. E. B. Du Bois On Sociology and the Black Community.* Chicago: The University of Chicago Press, 1978.

Hamilton, Virginia. *W. E. B. Du Bois.* New York: HarperCollins Publishers, 1972.

Heckscher, August. *Woodrow Wilson.* New York: Charles Scribner's Sons, 1991.

Horne, Gerald. *Black & Red: W. E. B. Du Bois and the Afro-American Response to the Cold War, 1944-1963.* Albany, NY: State University of New York Press, 1986.

Hubbard, Dolan, ed. *The Souls of Black Folk: One Hundred Years Later.* Columbia: University of Missouri Press, 2003.

Kellogg, Charles Flint. *NAACP: A History of the National Association for the Advancement of Colored People, 1909-*

*1920*. Baltimore: The Johns Hopkins Press, 1967.

Lewis, David Levering. *W. E. B. Du Bois: The Fight For Equality and the American Century, 1919-1963*. New York: Henry Holt and Company, 2000.

―――. *W. E. B. Du Bois: Biography of a Race, 1868-1919*. New York: Henry Holt and Company, 1993.

Marable, Manning. *W. E. B. Du Bois: Black Radical Democrat*. Boston: Twayne Publishers, 1986.

Meier, August. *Negro Thought in America, 1880-1915*. Ann Arbor: The University of Michigan Press, 1964.

Moon, Henry Lee. *The Emerging Thought of W. E. B. Du Bois*. New York: Simon and Schuster, 1972.

Ovington, Mary White. *The Walls Came Tumbling Down*. New York: Harcourt, Brace and Company, 1947.

Rudwick, Elliot. *W. E. B. Du Bois: A Study in Minority Group Leadership*. Philadelphia: University of Pennsylvania Press, 1960.

Tolnay, Stewart and E. M. Beck. *A Festival of Violence: An Analysis of Southern Lynchings, 1882-1930*. Urbana: University of Illinois Press, 1995.

Tuttle, William Jr., ed. *W. E. B. Du Bois*. Englewood Cliffs, NJ: Prentice Hall, Inc., 1973.

Weinberg, Meyer, ed. *W. E. B. Du Bois: A Reader*. New York: Harper & Row, Publishers, 1970.

Weinstein, Allen and Frank Otto Gatell, eds. *The Segregation Era 1863-1954: A Modern Reader*. New York: Oxford University Press, 1970.

White, Walter. *A Man Called White: The Autobiography of Walter White*. New York: The Viking Press, 1948.

Zangrando, Robert. *The NAACP Crusade Against Lynching, 1909-1950*. Philadelphia: Temple University Press, 1980.

# Web sites

http://www.library.umass.edu/spcoll/dubois.html
An archive of papers and photographs related to W. E. B. Du Bois held at the University of Massachusetts at Amherst.

http://www.thecrisismagazine.com/
The online site of the NAACP's magazine *The Crisis.*

http://www.naacp.org/
The official Web site of the National Association for the Advancement of Colored People.

http://www.fas.harvard.edu/~du_bois/
The official Web site of the W. E. B. Du Bois Institute for African and African American Research at Harvard University.

# Index